CREATING WOMEN'S NETWORKS

CREATING WOMEN'S NETWORKS

A How-To Guide for Women and Companies

Catalyst

Foreword by Sheila W. Wellington

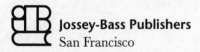

Jossey-Bass Publishers
San Francisco

Jossey-Bass books and products are available through most bookstores. To contact Jossey-Bass
directly, call (888) 378–2537, fax to (800) 605–2665, or visit our website at www.josseybass.com.

Substantial discounts on bulk quantities of Jossey-Bass books are available to corporations, professional associations, and other organizations. For details and discount information, contact the
special sales department at Jossey-Bass.

 Manufactured in the United States of America on Lyons Falls Turin Book. This paper is acid-free
and 100 percent totally chlorine-free.

Library of Congress Cataloging-in-Publication Data

Creating women's networks : a how-to guide for women and companies
/ Catalyst ; foreword by Sheila Wellington. — 1st ed.
    p. cm. — (The Jossey-Bass business & management series)
Includes index.
ISBN 0-7879-4014-3 (acid-free paper)
  1. Business networks. 2. Women — Social networks.
3. Businesswomen. I. Catalyst, inc. II. Series.
HD69.S8 C74 1999
658.4'09'082—dc21

                             98-40255

FIRST EDITION
HB Printing   10 9 8 7 6 5 4 3 2 1

CONTENTS

Foreword xi

Sheila W. Wellington

Acknowledgments xiii

Introduction 1

Network Snapshot: Coming Together from Around the World:
  Bankers Trust 9

PART ONE: BEGINNINGS 11

1 Do You Need a Network? 13

2 The Right Roles and Goals for Your Network 29

Network Snapshot: A Business Initiative That Reaches Beyond Members:
  Texas Instruments 43

3 On Your Mark, Get Set: Getting Organized and Started 45

Network Snapshot: An Oasis in Financial Services: Dain Rauscher 55

PART TWO: IT'S UP AND RUNNING, NOW WHAT? 57

4 Want Real Power? Build Companywide Support 59

5 You've Arrived! Putting Your Plans into Action 85

Network Snapshot: Growing from the Grass Roots: 3M 117

6 Stay Focused! Keeping on Track as the Network Ages 119

7 What If You Face Real Problems? How to Make Them
   Conquerable Challenges 142

Network Snapshot: CEO Support from the Beginning: Kodak 157

Epilogue 159

RESOURCES

A Catalyst's Summary Findings from the Women's Workplace
   Network Survey 161

B Examples from Women's Networks

   1 Dow Chemical WIN Change Process 171

   2 Bausch & Lomb's Diversity Checklist 173

   3 Kodak Employees Briefing Book: Selected Items
      from a Network Guide 175

   4 Kimberly-Clark Employee Network Descriptions 179

INDEX 181

RESEARCH REPORTS 185

FOREWORD

O ne of the most striking changes in the United States in the last fifty years has been women's entry into the workforce. In 1950, women amounted to only 29.6 percent of the workforce. By 1997, they were up to 46 percent. And the proportion is only increasing. In fact, estimates are that between 1996 and 2006, women will account for 59 percent of total labor force growth.

The picture looks very different, however, as you move up the organizational ladder. Women have been tremendously successful in entering the workforce and gaining footholds in entry-level and mid-management positions. But look toward the top of most companies. The makeup of that group of leaders hasn't changed nearly as much in fifty years. In 1996, women represented slightly more than 10 percent of the corporate officers in the Fortune 500. Look at the top five earners in each of these companies, as Catalyst does in its annual *Census of Corporate Officers and Top Earners,* and the number drops to 3 percent.

In some companies, though, the picture looks a lot brighter. Women are represented not only among entry-level positions and at the middle managerial levels but at the top managerial levels as well—and among vice presidents, executive vice presidents, and even presidents and CEOs. What's happening there?

These corporations and firms have recognized that paying attention to business means paying attention to the changing workforce. Women now represent a substantial proportion of the talent pool from which companies draw their employees and the potential customers for their services and products. Ignoring over half the working and buying population is a bad business decision.

How do these top companies do it? They employ a wide range of strategies to recruit women, to retain women, to develop women, and to promote qualified women. They understand the opportunities that come with having women at all levels in their workforce, as well as the challenges women face in corporate America. They respond to the career development needs, work/life balance needs, and networking needs of women in their organizations. In so doing, they ensure the recruitment and retention of a talented and loyal workforce.

How can women themselves make this happen? They can come together in their organization—first, to identify and help each other gain the skills and experience they need to be successful; second, to educate top management and other employees about women's contributions to and concerns about their workplace; third, to share their knowledge about the informal norms of the company and subtle advancement strategies; and fourth, to help their company succeed by tapping women's talents. To do all this, women are working together, forming groups of like-minded employees who can help each other move their careers and their organizations forward. That is how women's networks come into being.

We at Catalyst have drawn on our more than thirty years of experience to put *Creating Women's Networks* together. It is designed to give you the tools you need to start a network of your own and set it on a course for success throughout its life span. I'm sure you look forward to getting started, so—read on.

September 1998
New York, New York

Sheila W. Wellington
President, Catalyst

ACKNOWLEDGMENTS

This book is the product of work with women's workplace networks by Catalyst over the past fifteen years. It was conceived by Catalyst President Sheila W. Wellington in conjunction with the astute thinking of Cedric Crocker and Susan Williams, editors at Jossey-Bass, with the latter steering the project at Jossey-Bass. Betty Spence oversaw the writing and editing from the Catalyst side.

Special thanks go to Tara Levine, who drafted this book. Without her extensive knowledge of networks there would be no book. Carol Wheeler masterfully and rapidly created the final draft. Marcia Brumit Kropf was deeply involved with the project from its inception, and Bickley Townsend oversaw the research project. Thanks also to Laura O'Loughlin, who reviewed drafts and contributed her years of experience with networks; and to Ellen Wernick, who helped organize our thinking and created easy-to-use approaches for encapsulating information. We are grateful also to Carrie Lane, who set up and conducted interviews of women's network leaders, and to Debbie Zarlin, who prepared the manuscript for the publisher.

We would also like to thank Karen Sharpe, whose developmental work helped us refine our focus. Thanks especially to Susan Williams, who believes in our mission and whose dedication, insight, and patience have brought us closer to its realization.

We also thank the network leaders and others who found time in their tight schedules to share the ups and downs of their networks. Most of all, we salute the women's networks included in this book—and those we may not yet know about—for their work at supporting and encouraging our nation's corporate women. Long may they thrive!

CREATING WOMEN'S NETWORKS

INTRODUCTION

Women Helping Women • Women Helping Their Employers
That's a Women's Network

Women's networks are a phenomenon that grew out of the overlapping need of companies to reach out to the women in their organization and the critical need of women to reach out to each other.

You probably don't need Catalyst to tell you that in many organizations, women can feel isolated and out of the loop. Many women tell us of being in offices where the men often go out to lunch together or stop off for a drink after work. Women tend to find that informality with men more difficult to achieve; they are not usually at those lunches or after-work gatherings. Yet the information shared during those "down times" is important, and if women want to gain access to it, they need to join in those activities.

But women also need to network with other women, to gain information that only other women know, such as how to navigate their workplace's waters *as women*. However, that often requires some effort: there are usually fewer women working together and they often have constraints—child-care issues, for instance—that men devote less attention to. There are often too few women in management in a particular company for them to form a critical mass in any one division or department or office. To work together for their common good, to have an impact on the organization, even to get to know each other, they must take active steps to get together—and that means a formal network.

Loosely defined, a women's network is a group of women in an organization, formed to act as a resource for members and the company. It can be formal or informal, made up of fifty women or five hundred women. The point is that these networks are there to help the women in the company—and to help the company itself. The mission statements of a few groups speak for themselves:

WIN—Women's Interactive Network (Kimberly-Clark)

The mission of WIN is to support Kimberly-Clark in achieving growth and profitability objectives by championing the organization's efforts to capitalize on the talents and contributions of its women employees.

Women in Management network (McGraw-Hill)

The mission of the Women in Management network is to enhance the value of the McGraw-Hill companies by capitalizing on the skills and expertise of women in management.

Women's Advisory Council (3M)

The Women's Advisory Council provides women's perspectives on workplace issues and helps create an environment where all employees can contribute fully to the success of 3M.

Women's Network (Texas Instruments)

Our mission is to have a culture that values and utilizes diversity at all levels, provides equitable opportunities and develops the full potential of each employee to make Texas Instruments a world leader in productivity and profitability.

Why Have a Women's Network At All?

Like most great ideas, networks arose out of a gaping hole: there were needs that were not being fulfilled. Most women's networks form to address these three problem areas:

- First, the overall company environment often includes built-in assumptions that are more of a burden for women than for men. Women need to join together to bring these assumptions into the open and help the company adapt to the real requirements of modern life.

- Second, company social structures tend to isolate women, making it hard for them to rely on each other for advice and support. Women need to come together to share strategies and help each other overcome this isolation.
- Third, established career paths can sometimes exclude women. Women need to get together to focus on their own career development and the development of women at other levels in the organization.

Do these concerns sound important to you? Would achieving goals like those we mention be worth the effort you might have to expend? Are you eager to get started in that direction? Or are women in your organization pressing you to support their efforts to do so? If so, you've come to the right place. This book is intended to serve as your guide to the formation and maintenance of an effective and productive women's network in virtually any business environment.

What Do Women's Networks Do?

To address the three problem areas, networks commonly take action on several fronts: they advise senior management, often through Human Resources or a diversity council, on the issues facing women in the company; they hold networking events for members; they set up mentoring programs and speakers series; and they do many other things as well. Each project or program addresses one of the three problem areas, and there are often overlaps. Obviously, as you improve the environment for women on an individual basis, you improve the environment for women overall, and, of most interest to the company, improving the environment for women improves the environment for all employees.

What Makes a Women's Network Happen?

The spark can come from a variety of places:

Sometimes it's a few women meeting to talk about what's happening at work. The talk flows fast and furious, and one woman says, to general agreement, "This is great. Let's get together more often!" Soon the mailing list starts to grow, and they have the beginnings of a formal network.

Or it might be one particular event that leads to a revelation. Perhaps a lot of promotions go through and not one of the new titles is held by a woman. Or someone goes to a meeting, looks around at the participants, and sees how few women are there—then realizes that meetings are often like this.

Or the CEO or an executive might begin thinking, "We're missing out on a lot of talent. We need to know more about what's going on with women here," and get the senior women together to figure out how to find out.

Sometimes it's the result of a question asked at the annual meeting about women's opportunities at the company. And sometimes it's an exodus of women from the organization that wakes up women and top management to the need to reach out to women in the company.

Whatever the reason, women's networks work. They are one of the best ways for women to get the career advice and support they want, and for the company to get the most out of one of its most important assets.

What Real Impact Do Women's Networks Have?

You may still feel a bit skeptical—after all, there's been a great deal of talk about networking over the years, but is it really useful? What does this sort of group actually *do* for the network members and for the company? Investment firm Dain Rauscher knows networks are good for business. The company's Association of Women Brokers made a promise to its CEO that if Dain Rauscher supported the women's network, the network members would, in turn, make themselves better brokers. As a result of the network's mentoring programs, career development opportunities, and annual conference, sales for women's network members have increased by 19.2 percent, 5 percent more than for the rest of the firm. Female brokers attribute the advantage to their membership in the network. That's just one example of network success—and we'll offer many more throughout this book.

There is a tremendous impact on the members themselves:

> For the women who have been involved in the network, it's been very much of a confidence-building, transformational kind of experience. It's been critical to the members.
>
> —*Women's network leader*

> I look at it as personal growth. You are getting experience and knowledge that is unsurpassed. It provides business experience and growth experience for women that you don't get in the workplace when you're not in a management position.
>
> —*Women's network leader*

There is also a tremendous impact on the company:

I can't imagine our culture functioning without the women's group. That's the strength of their impact.

—Senior vice president

We've really been instrumental in changing the culture. When I started, there were very few women who were doing any sort of flexible work arrangement. Five years later, we have over four hundred people working flexibly, and they're not all women. There are quite a few men with flexible hours. So we are proud that we are slowly but surely getting the message through.

—Women's network leader

There are a lot of good people in this organization and I need to find them. Through the network's mentoring program and networking events, I have access to people when I'm thinking about advancement and succession planning.

—Management liaison

How Does Catalyst Support Women's Networks?

Catalyst has long recognized the potential of these groups for effecting change for women and for companies. As the premier resource for information and advice on women's networks, Catalyst has worked with women's networks from all regions and all industries for over fifteen years. In 1988 Catalyst published *Building an Effective Corporate Women's Group*, which examines the origins, structure, and purpose of these groups. Since then, Catalyst has provided networks with concrete advice and acted as the national link among these networks. This book distills the lessons we have learned to date.

Where Are the Networks?

Catalyst has seen many changes in women's networks over time. Most important, their numbers are increasing. Currently, at least 33 percent of Fortune 100 companies have women's networks. Even a partial list of corporations and firms in which women's networks exist reads like an honor roll of big business:

Ford

IBM

Hewlett-Packard

Procter & Gamble

Motorola

Merck

Dow Chemical

American Stores

Xerox

3M

Eastman Kodak

Texas Instruments

Bankers Trust

McDonald's

Kraft

McGraw-Hill

These networks often operate with a great deal of senior-level support. Many senior executives advise women's networks, or are even the creators of the network in their organization. Women's networks are more likely than ever to be formal advisers to the company on women's issues, and they often link into other diversity efforts that are under way.

One of the most important trends is that senior women in companies are increasingly starting or participating in women's networks. This visible and active support is something new—until recently, it was believed to be unwise for a woman at or near the top to take a visible role in addressing gender issues. It appears that, finally, the career risks associated with openly supporting women's networks have decreased—a phenomenon that can probably be attributed to the slow but steady increase in numbers of women at the top.

What Does *Creating Women's Networks* Offer?

In this book Catalyst shares the learning it has gained through interactions with women's networks over the last fifteen years and in a two-year research study. That study included a series of five roundtable discussions with over fifty leaders of women's networks across the country, interviews with management liaisons at twenty-one of those companies, and a national survey of women's networks. This is the largest data-gathering process on this topic to date, and one that resulted in a rich trove and varied base of information. See Resource A for a summary of the specific findings from the study. The body of this book presents that data in usable form: the information, advice, best practices, and case studies that will simplify the process of starting, maintaining, reviving, or revising a women's network in any organization.

Creating Women's Networks provides step-by-step, hands-on advice on creating a network or working with a network already in existence. Think of it as your own personal networking expert, an expert always at your beck and call, ready at a moment's notice to guide you through the peaks and pitfalls of network creation.

The book follows the life cycle of a network. Part One starts at the beginning, when a network forms and members are deciding purpose and activities. We outline the steps you can take in understanding the company environment as well as the needs of members in the network. We then move into the critical area of building support for the network, a step that is most important, and one that ensures the long-term success of the group. We then review how to get your activities and programs off the ground. This is the fun part. Seeing your plans in action is exhilarating and makes all the planning beforehand worth it. Part Two moves into the ongoing life of the network—from developing initial support to dealing with necessary changes, including making the transition into a different network or out of existence altogether.

Depending on where your network is in its life, you can focus on the chapters that seem most appropriate. However, whatever stage the network is in, we suggest you take a look at the whole book. The critical processes outlined throughout—such as defining goals and strategies and building support—are often the ones women's networks find themselves going back to over and over, no matter how many years they've been around.

Each section includes examples of networks in the appropriate phase of their life cycle, to give you a living, breathing sense of what networks are like in action. Each chapter begins with the guiding questions for the phase of network life it addresses, and ends with a checklist to help network organizers cover all the bases when they put the concepts into practice. The chapters also include a rundown of the pitfalls commonly encountered at each stage of the process. Placed strategically throughout the book are five Network Snapshots: portraits of long-running and extremely successful women's networks from a range of American industries. And at every turn, you'll hear from two sets of people with front-line experience with networks like the one this book is designed to help develop: network leaders (the women who organize and run the networks) and management liaisons (the people in management who advise and champion networks). They will serve as your guides throughout the process.

As an organization that has been working in the forefront of women's advancement issues for more than three decades, Catalyst is particularly pleased to be able share its expertise with a wide audience. We look forward to helping you as you create your network or work on making your current network better.

COMING TOGETHER FROM AROUND THE WORLD: BANKERS TRUST

Origins. Global Partnership for Women had a classic grassroots beginning at Bankers Trust, a highly decentralized organization. Four or five women managers from different Bankers Trust locations met at a company-sponsored training course in 1991 and decided to stay in touch. Drawing on their personal "mini-networks," these initiators actually got a companywide women's network going that same year.

Support. At the very beginning, the core group presented a page-and-a-half proposal to the president of Bankers Trust, who responded with his full support and told them to "go global." The group has had a clear commitment from senior management ever since, and support from middle management is increasingly evident.

Membership. As of 1998, Global Partnership has six hundred members. Both men and women belong, although most events are geared toward women. Many members are from HR, with which the network has a close relationship. The network has no trouble getting new members, which leaders attribute to strong communications, including word of mouth.

Leadership Structure. The network has no formal structure of accountability; it describes its leadership as fluid and democratic. There is no voting and there are no elections, but there is a steering committee made up of members from each of the firm's business areas. Because active leaders are often selected for high-profile assignments overseas, it is sometimes a challenge to maintain a high-energy steering committee, but new leaders usually step up quickly. The group is not interested in creating a hierarchy of leadership, finding it is preferable that more people gain the benefits of developmental leadership opportunities.

Goals and Successes. The network originally had three goals: trading business information, accomplishing some informal networking, and providing women with female role models from senior management. Members arranged networking breakfasts at which seven or eight women met with a senior woman. It was the first time senior women had been called upon in this way and they loved it.

The second phase of the network was the communications phase. At the time, the women's network was the sole place where all employees could meet with and listen to senior management. Five hundred people—both women and men— showed up at one network event to hear a talk by the firm's chairman.

The next network project was helping employees develop skills, with an emphasis on what organizers referred to as "women-related" skills. Speakers and events were geared toward teaching presentation skills, the fine art of taking credit for your work, communications between men and women, and the like.

Major Success. The most recent, and continuing, project of Global Partnership is expanding the network and its goals to women outside the firm, with a view to creating a community of women in investment management. The network is rightly very proud of its annual "Women on Wall Street" session, which in 1997 drew 1,600 partici-

pants. Many clients or potential clients who were there sent letters to BT's chairman praising the event, and, more important, proving that the network contributes directly to the bottom line.

Activities and Programs. The network has an interactive Web site with e-mail and video conferencing. It does extensive community outreach, including clothing drives and mentoring for local teens and students. It holds networking forums and seminars, and the early breakfasts have turned into mentoring lunches where women meet with senior leadership.

Membership Benefits. Many women have found new jobs (through both lateral and vertical moves) and others have found contacts in different areas of the organization, a major plus in a large firm as decentralized as Bankers Trust. In a predominantly male environment, the network allows women to work with each other while contributing to the corporate culture through unique events and activities.

Advisory Role. The network does not advise management or HR in any formal way, but it is an important voice in the company. In fact, HR often picks up on the network's momentum and implements ideas that surface through the network. When the firm hit a rough place a few years ago, the network was instrumental in boosting sagging morale—it organized breakfasts at which the new management team met with twenty to thirty employees at a time to discuss changes. Eventually, every employee met with the new leaders, and Bankers Trust's retention rate was higher than expected.

PART ONE

BEGINNINGS

Women's networks come in all shapes and sizes—the possibilities are limitless. Networks can focus on almost anything within the company. That creates many opportunities but it also presents what could be a rather alarming challenge. This guidebook is designed to help potential network organizers—and the managers and HR departments of their companies—move confidently and comfortably ahead with setting up the sort of network that will be most beneficial to the women of the company and to the company as a whole.

The first three chapters are oriented toward people who are just beginning to set up networks. The advice presented here can also be useful for existing women's networks, however; the same lessons that apply to new networks can be useful in refocusing a network that has been in existence for years.

Chapter One: Do You Need a Network? A network doesn't exist in a vacuum—it must have a purpose. This chapter covers the preliminary steps involved in seeing whether there is sufficient interest to get started, selecting the core group and surveying potential sources of support within the organization, and then making a detailed survey to find out what needs the network can respond to and how you can gather essential information about the environment in which the network operates.

Chapter Two: The Right Roles and Goals for Your Network. Who will belong to the network? What will its agenda be? The group needs a focused plan that it can communicate clearly to others in the organization, and that requires definition of the network's role in the company—is it to be advisory or programmatic or both, for instance? If this phase is handled well, the result is clear timetables, accountabilities, and satisfactory results. Often, successful networks make this planning process an annual event, reviewing the past year's achievements and deciding what the network will focus on in the coming year. In that way, at the same time that they celebrate their past successes, members develop a clear idea of where the network is going next.

Chapter Three: On Your Mark, Get Set. Systems—agreed-upon structures and strategies by which groups work—are needed to make sure the network functions effectively. Network organizers often overlook this step in the excitement of creation. However, few things are more important to network success than a structure to ensure the work gets done and a clear communications strategy to make sure the organization knows who you are, and this chapter outlines the steps that will get you to that point.

CHAPTER ONE

DO YOU NEED A NETWORK?

Guiding Questions: What do you want to accomplish through this network? How can you design the network's mission, activities, and structure to achieve those goals? What is the culture of your organization? How do you pinpoint the needs a network can fulfill?

First of all, obviously, to form a women's network, you need women. And before you can continue, you need the initiators—a core group to sign on to the project. Generally speaking, six to ten people is ideal—large enough to get the job done without going into overload; not so large that efficiency and manageability are difficult to maintain.

Because this stage is so crucial to how the network unfolds (and even to if it does), the organizers need to select the core group carefully. Four aspects of each individual—commitment, skills, diversity, and collegiality—should be considered:

• *Commitment:* Initiators need to be prepared to devote a fair amount of time to the project, and it will certainly help if they are dedicated to the cause. There will surely be triumphs and rewards, but, inevitably, there will also be delays and setbacks. Women who are gung-ho for the network but too swamped to spare any time for it won't fit in at this stage, though they can certainly be useful as sounding boards and resources. They can provide quick feedback on how developing network plans seem likely to affect their own job areas, for instance.

• *Skills:* Interpersonal skills are truly crucial for working in a small group like this. And over and above the basic ability to work and play well with others, each member of the core group needs to be able to ask good questions and listen well—those are the key skills for conducting interviews, focus groups, and brainstorming sessions. The core group also needs collective knowledge of how the company works, how it operates, and who makes it happen—no one person can know it all, obviously, but you need women who can fill in for each other on various departments and functions. It's also useful to have at least one member who has studied the process of developing questionnaires and interpreting the results accurately.

• *Diversity:* It's critical to have a broad representation in your core group of different areas and levels of the company (unless you plan to exclude certain levels from your network; see Chapter Two), as well as of different ethnic backgrounds and ages—not only so you'll get a clear picture of what's happening all over the workplace and what issues matter to different segments, but also to make it clear that the network represents women throughout the company.

• *Collegiality:* It's essential that your core group work well together. This is a matter of intent as well as skill—people who can work well with others don't always choose to do so, and don't always find it possible to work well with everyone they encounter. You need a group that clicks. The members don't all have to agree on every detail—diversity of opinion, even disagreement, can help you and the network learn and grow. You just all have to respect each other's opinions and be able to figure out how to resolve your differences.

First Steps

The group you form now may well evolve into a steering committee for the whole network. But for now, it will be spending most of its time gathering information.

Assessing the Environment

To get some preliminary feeling for how supportive your company actually is of women, you can ask yourselves some questions and come up with some answers. About career development programs, say:

• Is career development a priority for your company?
• Are there formal systems for advancement?
• Are there women at the higher levels of authority?
• Is there a mentoring program?

   Or about flexible work arrangements:

• Is there a formal policy in this area?
• Can employees work part time without sacrificing their careers?
• Do you find flexible work arrangements in all areas and levels of the company?

Catalyst Counts

One question you might not think to ask: Among senior women, how many are in line positions (anything with bottom-line responsibility, such as sales); how many in staff (human resources, public relations, and other support functions)? It's just being widely recognized how important that division is—between line and staff—to the division of power and responsibility in a company. And that recognition is coming about largely due to Catalyst research. *The Catalyst Census of Corporate Officers and Top Earners,* for example, showed that such higher-ups are largely drawn from people in line positions, so if there are few women holding those positions in your company, you know that for women to reach the highest levels, something more than sheer hard work is needed.

That *Census* and other Catalyst research—for example, our 1998 report on dual-career couples *(Two Careers, One Marriage)* or our study of part-time professionals *(A New Approach to Flexibility: Managing the Work/Time Equation)*—could be helpful to you in thinking about your workplace, as well as in formulating goals and avenues of investigation. If you'd like to obtain copies, see the note at the end of the book for contact information.

In any case, even if, after asking yourselves these questions and many more, you find that the answers add up to a gratifyingly favorable grade for your company, it is Catalyst's firm belief that you and your company will benefit from having a women's network. Catalyst believes that a women's network is a vital component of a working environment in which women participate as fully as men. Not only are networks crucial to women's advancement, but more important, they have the power to make change happen, something all companies need in these fast-changing times, even if they don't recognize it.

Gauging Potential Support

A network's success depends on companywide support, but it's unlikely you'll get that at once. You might find strong support in one area and indifference in another. But don't worry, the level of support is far from immutable; it will vary over time (in a favorable direction if all goes according to plan). Networks have three major constituencies:

Women. As the network grows and more women in the company learn about it, momentum builds, and the atmosphere may become more positive. To assess the interest of women in general, ask yourself a few questions:

- Do women talk among themselves about gender-related issues, such as how few women are promoted or whether women are sufficiently represented in senior management?
- Are there many women around after hours?
- Do many women turn up for any informal networking activities your company may sponsor, such as a brown-bag lunch or a seminar on career advancement?

Management. Clearly, management support is pretty essential if you want your network's plans brought to fruition. While networks offer management many benefits, management also has concerns, including the fear that a network will focus women's resentment against the status quo and that time devoted to the network takes time away from the job itself. It's up to network organizers, of course, to allay those fears and show how the network can increase productivity and make advancement opportunities available to everyone. (See Chapter Four for more on building support.) The very best kind of support you can get is from senior leadership.

If you or any of your cohort know of any company leaders who have spoken out on gender or work/life issues, by the way, you will want to enlist them in your cause as soon as possible. Speak to them early and consistently as your plans form. Their advice will be invaluable.

Human Resources. This department has many of the same goals that a women's network has, and it often welcomes a network for that very reason. Unfortunately, there is sometimes resistance from Human Resources because HR staff fear that the formation of a network implies that they have fallen down on the job. Those fears must also be laid to rest, by all of you initiators making it very clear that you wish to work in partnership with HR and explaining from the first how the department can help you while you are helping it.

Getting Off the Ground

In fact, one of the first things a women's network initiator should do is have an informal talk with someone in Human Resources (if you have someone in your group who works in HR, so much the better). Perhaps the simplest way is to just walk into an HR person's office and say, "What do you think of this? This is what we'd like to do. . . ." Concentrate on being nonthreatening—such forays are sometimes taken poorly and you want to do all you can to have HR on your side, especially when you begin gathering company data.

The Risk Factor

Catalyst has never seen anyone passed over for a promotion or terminated because they got together to form a network. Nevertheless, in certain companies, women interested in forming a network have decided to go about it very slowly. Often these women will confine themselves at first to informal meetings outside the office environment and outside working hours.

One network at a large corporation passed around a clipboard to women employees, for signing up for network meetings. They found that a lot of women wouldn't sign up because the method was too public. One network had just been a "dinner network" for many years. Eventually Human Resources asked them if they would turn their group into a formal network. HR knew about it, of course, because there were HR women in the informal network all along.

Ask yourself what will happen in your culture. There are great benefits accruing from a women's network, especially if you are one of its initiators. Yet it is a public statement, and it's sometimes hard for women, often senior women especially, to take what they perceive as a chance, separating themselves from their cohorts on the basis of being women. A careful assessment of your own environment is always the best plan.

Of course, if there are already other networks in your company, the ground has been prepared and you're unlikely to encounter major resistance to your plans. The other networks will probably offer to help, in fact, as well as being willing to work with you on joint projects.

Assessing the Climate

The first step in solving a problem is figuring out exactly what the problem is. Similarly, before a network can come into its own, its members need to understand what's going on in their organization. That's where the climate survey comes in. *Climate survey* is a term that refers to the process of identifying the opportunities that exist for the network, as well as the challenges it will face. In other words, it's a snapshot of the environment, or climate, in which the women's network is operating. Rather than creating activities based on what you *think* to be the case, you create the network based on what you *know* to be the case.

Information the Network Needs

A climate survey can be broken out into three areas:

- The issues facing women in your organization and the opportunities you want to create for those women.
- The environment in which the network is operating—the level of support the network has and the interest in these issues on the part of managers, executives, and Human Resources.
- The interests of the network members as well as the constraints they may be operating under (the time and energy they can commit to the network).

Later in this chapter, you will find sample questions for each segment of your company's climate. But how do you gather all this information?

First you must decide who will do the gathering. Typically, even if there is a large group of eager new networkers, a small group of six to ten members can co-ordinate this process and report back to the larger group. The process can take a month or longer, depending on how exhaustive the data-gathering process is. If possible, include women with research backgrounds to coordinate the effort—many companies have research and analysis functions, and the skills used in those areas will be most useful to this endeavor.

You may already be working with Human Resources, which can be an important source of information. HR staff know whether the company already has the information you need—and if you need more, they can help you get it. Some companies, though, are very hesitant to release employee survey responses, high-level statistics, and the like. Don't be discouraged if that's the case in your workplace. There is plenty of information that's readily available when you know how to recognize it.

That's where Chart 1.1 comes in. Use it as a guide to gathering information in all kinds of ways from all kinds of sources. You probably know how to do much of this already, but a chart is an easy way to look at things systematically. We hope it will give you a grasp of the various methods of learning about your own company culture. But you're the only one who can decide what kind of data you need and how much time you have to devote to these efforts, and remember, you don't have to gather all the data now. Learning is a continuous process—and you'll be learning (and your company will be changing) throughout the life of your network.

Catalyst's advice: Start small, perhaps with some informal conversations with members or senior women. Use that as the base for further analysis. Remember that *quantitative* data (facts and numbers) are best used to reinforce the range of issues raised or show the broad-based support for an effort, while *qualitative* data (descriptions and interviews) can give you a deeper understanding of the texture of the issues raised and of the detailed experiences of participants. You'll get the most

Chart 1.1 Climate Survey Tools and Tips

Qualitative Tool—Talking It Over	Why and When to Use It	Drawbacks	Energy Needed
Informal brainstorming among network members	• This is often the best way to start. Here questions about the network can emerge, as well as concerns about how to go about getting data. Such discussions ensure that all your efforts reflect network members' interests and needs.	• These discussions alone won't be enough. You need to draw from a wider base to make sure the credibility of the data is strong.	• Relatively little. Someone must call the meeting itself, summarize the results, and report them back to participants, but none of these need be difficult or time-consuming.
Individual conversations with selected network members, senior managers, senior women at the company, or other involved parties	• These are the "confidential" conversations that can result in frank talk about the environment for women and the network. • You can sell the network and its importance and develop relationships with senior-level supporters who can be formal and informal champions of the network. • You can also gain access to senior women's knowledge of the company and get tips from them on how the network should proceed. • Be prepared with detailed questions on the topic you'll be discussing.	• Pick and choose your interviews carefully. You may not have a great deal of information prepared yet about the network, and thus you may want to skip known skeptics and return to them once you have a clear action agenda and next steps you can point to. • Remember, this is a business meeting like any other. You will be unlikely to gain much information unless you reinforce the importance of your subjects' opinions and ideas, and the confidentiality of the discussion.	• This is a more time-consuming process because of the prep time required to target interviewees, prepare yourself and them for the interview, and then complete the post-interview summaries and thank yous. • If you find a potential supporter or champion of the network, the work doesn't end with the completion of the interview. Maintaining the flow of information on network activities is critical to retaining friends and supporters of the network.
Focus groups of selected individuals or representatives of targeted groups	• You can reach a range of employees or employee groups at the same time.	• In pulling together a group of ten to fifteen people for a focus group, you	• This is the most complicated of the qualitative tools, and requires the

(continued)

Chart 1.1 Continued

Qualitative Tool—Talking It Over	Why and When to Use It	Drawbacks	Energy Needed
	• Perfect for looking at a specific function or set of issues. For example, if you're trying to understand the issues for women in operations, you could hold a focus group of women from various levels in that function.	need to be ready for the discussions generated by the invitation. Be prepared to explain why you are gathering this information and how it will be used. • Confidentiality can be a concern with these groups, especially if you have too many participants, or if they don't know each other. Reiterate the need for confidentiality during the discussions.	most energy. The logistics to set up a focus group can be significant—targeting participants, reserving space, creating a question summary, reporting findings to participants. The best approach is to share responsibility for using this tool among two or three people who can divide up logistics work and even share leadership of the focus group itself.
Quantitative Tool—Counting Up	**Why and When to Use It**	**Drawbacks**	**Energy Needed**
Analysis of Human Resources data	• The general rule: take advantage of any data you can get. It is invaluable to be able to show the numbers of women in senior positions, in line versus staff positions, in career development programs, or resigning. Such numbers give you a picture of what's going on and help you prioritize issues. Numbers are powerful; they can raise awareness and alert others to little-known problems.	• You need to be sure you understand the numbers you are given and what they represent. Human Resources data may not be the easiest to decipher, and you don't want to misread the information. Be sure to ask for help from the data management office in Human Resources. • Also be sure to combine this quantitative data with the qualitative data you have. Use one to test the other.	• Depending on the amount of data you have, this can be a relatively time-intensive process. Target the top five areas you'd like to understand better, and then conduct analyses accordingly.

Chart 1.1 Continued

Quantitative Tool— Counting Up	Why and When to Use It	Drawbacks	Energy Needed
	• The data may be seen as confidential or the company may simply be reluctant to share them. Try for the numbers, but don't be surprised if you don't get them. • If you can't get Human Resources data, you can still compile some numbers on your own. Start tracking the number of women in leadership positions, key women who leave the organization, and other numbers that are available to you.	For example, if you're seeing numbers indicating that women are leaving the company, do follow-up interviews with some of the women who have left to better understand their reasons for leaving.	
Formal surveys	• Formal surveys give you the opportunity to analyze data on a large number of individuals in a number of different ways—for example, looking at the differences in the responses of men and women. • Surveys can be used as a barometer of the issues facing many employees and their responses to them. • You can create a survey to use over time to gauge movement in	• Administering a formal survey to a relatively large population automatically boosts visibility for the network. If you aren't ready for the attention, then keep your survey small. You can choose to administer it just to network members, to women at a certain level, or even just to senior managers in a certain area. Prioritize the groups you need to best understand	• Written surveys require a great deal of work, mostly in the design and question-creation phase. Leverage any survey experience among network members or within the company to help you in this process. Another time-intensive portion is tabulating responses (by computer or by hand). Again, see if there are outside resources you can take advantage of.

(continued)

Chart 1.1 Continued

Quantitative Tool—Counting Up	Why and When to Use It	Drawbacks	Energy Needed
	certain areas. For example, as you create initiatives in coaching or mentoring, you can test the impact by looking at the responses to questions on those subjects year after year. • You can choose one of two options for your survey—creating your own allows you more flexibility in designing questions and you can have more questions. Adding questions to a companywide survey requires significantly less energy and reinforces the integration of the network with other companywide efforts.	and then target the survey accordingly.	

> ## Dual-Purpose Data: Keeping the "Business Case" in Mind
>
> Quantifying the network's potential impact on the organization is crucial—when you reinforce the bottom-line benefits of the women's network, you justify its existence to your company. As you gather your climate data, keep in mind what data you may need to make a business case for the network—that is, to show that it isn't just something that's nice to have, it's necessary. Business issues are customarily discussed in terms of numbers and the bottom line, so the more hard data you have, the stronger your argument will be. Quantitative figures such as representation of women at various levels of the organization, turnover rates, or even customer information cut by gender can all be very useful, and you may well find them during this phase.
>
> We'll go into this in much more detail in Chapter Four, but it's a good idea to start thinking in advance about the business case data you'll need. If you know what you want, you'll be more likely to recognize it when it appears—saving you time and energy later!

useful grounding—and the best information—when you balance those two perspectives.

How to Survey the Climate in Your Company

The goal at this stage is to understand the environment in which the network will operate. How do people in general—in top management—in middle management—in Human Resources—and women themselves—really feel about the role of women and their prospects in the company? Such attitudes aren't set in concrete; you'll be able to work on them as the network develops. But you do need a clear-eyed look at what you're up against.

It helps to picture the climate as falling somewhere along a continuum. At one extreme, an organization could enjoy a very high level of support for women's prospects—active champions among top management, willing partners in middle management and Human Resources, general understanding and almost instinctive acceptance at all levels. At the other extreme, support could be so low as to constitute active discouragement at every turn—distrust, dislike, suspicion. If you're contemplating the establishment of a network, your organization probably isn't quite at either end of the continuum; at the high end, everything you could want would already be happening out of sheer, joyous unanimity of spirit, and at the low end, such women as were employed would probably be too downtrodden to think of organizing. Most companies fall somewhere between moderately high and moderately low, and many have a medium level of support—acceptance of the concept in principle, cautious interest, a willingness to be shown that the effort is valuable to the company as well as to the women who take part.

To make things more complex—when were they ever simple?—there isn't one single climate to consider. The same organization can appear at different places on the overall continuum when approached from different viewpoints. A thoughtful preliminary survey explores the climate in three areas: the existing status of women in the company, the probable management reaction to formation of a network, and the market for the network among potential members. The following sections present more details and sample questions to help you survey the climate for each of these segments.

The Climate for Women. Understanding the needs of women in the company can be a daunting task. You can use a wide variety of data-gathering tools for this segment, but be prudent in your choices. Many networks gather data on this topic over several years. Don't try to learn everything in the first few months. Remember, the best approach is to start small, with interviews and discussions. You can go on from there to include broader tools such as surveys or Human Resources data.

> The most senior women in the organization decided that they wanted to address some of the issues involving women in the organization and what they did was reach out to women one or two levels below them and invite them to lunch. Each managing director took on a group of women. From those meetings they developed a task force, identified the issues that these women were struggling with, came up with recommendations. What they did was reach down and listen to find out what the issues were and then take care of them.
>
> —*Women's network leader*

Another way to target your information-gathering activities is to think about network membership (for help, see Chapter Two). If you think that network membership may be limited by level, geography, or function, then adjust your focus accordingly. If the anticipated membership will include all women, think about waves of data gathering. Start with the most easily accessible data and then expand outward.

A critical point to consider is the difference between what women need and what the network can provide. As you learn the answers to questions like those we have suggested, look at the options and make sure that the network isn't overestimating what it can do. Consider work/life balance, for example. Women face a variety of challenges in this area in most companies. Some things only company management can deal with, such as the need to formalize companywide policies on flexible work arrangements. Other things are well within the reach of an employee network—bringing in a speaker to discuss ways to implement flexible working arrangements effectively, for example. Still others can only be addressed at an individual level; each employee is personally responsible for taking advantage of flexible work options in a manner that serves the interests of both the company and the individual. What's needed is a three-way partnership among company management, the network, and the women who work in the company—none of the three can cover every aspect of a problem on its own.

The climate survey tools best suited to this area include informal conversations, interviews, focus groups, formal surveys, and benchmarking. It's also useful to analyze company data on women if you can get access to it.

Key Questions: Women in the Company

- What are the critical issues facing women in the organization today?
  Work/life balance? (flexible work arrangements, leaves, child care, elder care)
  Career development? (development and advancement opportunities, mentoring, lateral opportunities)
  Attitudinal issues? (understanding of gender issues, importance placed on women's issues in the organization)
- What could the women's network do to address those issues? (as opposed to action by the company and by women themselves)
- How do women stand in the company?
  What is the representation of women by level in the organization?
  Are women clustered in certain areas within the company?
  Are women of color represented at all levels of the organization? In what proportions?
  What proportion of women are in line positions? In staff positions?
  Are women represented fully in developmental programs, such as succession planning systems and training opportunities?
  What are the turnover rates of men compared to those of women?
  Is the company successful at recruiting women?
  How successful have initiatives targeted at gender been at the company?
- What has been the company's progress on these issues over time?
- What are other companies in your industry and region doing in this area?

The Climate for the Network. While Catalyst thinks that every company can and should have a women's network, not all companies would agree. As noted earlier, the responses to women's networks can range from open-armed acceptance through benign indifference to out-and-out hostility. Each environment requires a different approach to a network.

When we had our first meeting, we invited the top thirty-five women in the organization and about twenty showed up. The reason a lot of those women didn't show up was because it was a career risk to have your name associated with women's issues. So our very first agenda item was "Is the time right? Is the culture right? Are we ready?" And we were ready to end it at the very first meeting.

—Women's network leader

Networks operating in supportive environments can play an active role in advising management and Human Resources and can make themselves visible within the organization. Networks operating in a less supportive environment will need to move more slowly and focus on low-key networking events rather than larger, highly publicized events.

Either way, understanding the company climate will allow you to design your approach accordingly. The information-gathering process itself can reflect your general sense of how a network will be received. In addition to discussing these issues among network members, it also can prove wise to reach out to supportive senior women in the company, as they often are some of the best barometers of the company's response to a network. You can also reach out to other sympathetic senior managers who can act as advisers or mentors and give you a preview of how executives will react to the network.

The climate survey tools likely to prove most useful in this area include group member discussions, interviews with senior women in the company, and discussions with leaders or members of other employee networks. If you can arrange them, conversations with senior managers and executives will be invaluable—and if you can't, that will be a major finding in itself.

Key Questions: Company Climate for a Women's Network

- How will managers and executives view this network?
- Imagine that the network is already in place—what are some of the conversations happening around the organization? Among middle managers? Senior managers? Among women and men?
- What is the biggest challenge this network will face with respect to the organizational culture?
- What will the network need from managers and executives—financial support, visible support, meeting space, official sanction?
- What business case will you need to build in order to create support from groups within the organization?
- How important are women's issues at this organization?
- Are there other efforts currently under way that focus on gender? How have they been received?

- How comfortable would you feel as a member of a visible women's network?
- Think about potential members of this network—how supportive would their managers be of their participation in this network?
- Have there been other women's networks in the past? How has the company received them?
- Have there been other employee networks in the past? What was the company response?

The Climate Among Potential Members. To be a success, your network needs to align all activities and goals with member interests. In many networks, there are two levels of members: some who take an active role and others who choose only to attend events. You want to make sure that the approach and strategies of the network reflect the interests of both of these member groups. You always want to ask members, *"What do you want to get out of the network?"*

> You're competing for that woman's attention. She's got a job, she's got a family. If you don't demonstrate a benefit, you probably won't get her attention, you won't get her on your membership rolls, you won't get her at meetings.
>
> —*Women's network leader*

Learning the interests and needs of this population must be done in depth. Thus the best tools are often discussions among network members, brainstorming sessions, or one-on-one interviews with a cross-section of members. Another option is to create a short survey with questions about member interests and availability. Be sure to include some open-ended questions so that recipients have the opportunity to tell you more about their interests.

Key Questions: Network Members and Potential Members

- What are the three things you want to get out of this network?
- What do you need in order to justify your involvement in this network?
- How will your being a part of this network support the organization?
- Can your participation in this network help fulfill corporate objectives?
- What place do you want this network to have in the organization?
- If you were to describe the ideal impact this network would have on the organization, what would it be?
- Complete these two sentences: "The women's network will—" and "The women's network won't—"
- Realistically, how much time (weekly, monthly) can you devote to the network?
- How much time do you want to devote to the network?
- Do you see yourself taking on a leadership role within the network?

- Do you want to participate in committees?
- Would you prefer to limit your involvement to attendance at events?
- What other resources can you offer to the network? (Leveraging relationships with management, specific knowledge that will help the network, and so on.)

Checklist

☐ Decide to go ahead with establishing a women's network.

☐ Develop a core group.

☐ Do a preliminary assessment of the environment.

☐ Explore potential support from women in the organization and from top management and Human Resources.

☐ Assemble an internal team to assess the climate in the organization.

☐ Examine each of the three groupings—the climate for women at the company, for the network in the company, and for the network among potential members.

☐ Consider the range of data-gathering options available and choose appropriate tools given the issues, audiences, and time available for team members.

☐ Use the data-gathering efforts to gain a clear understanding of the current issues facing the network, its members, and the women in the organization.

☐ Determine the data that should be gathered on an ongoing basis in the future and the general time frame for the effort.

CHAPTER TWO

THE RIGHT ROLES AND GOALS FOR YOUR NETWORK

Guiding Question: How can a network that's raring to go focus its energy on just a few goals?

Once people decide to start a network, possibilities open in so many directions it can be distracting. The initial lists of goals beg to be translated into action—start a mentoring program, develop a speakers series, reach out to management, begin brown bag lunches for members—all *right now*. That energy is critical and will propel the network forward. But you have to be careful not to direct that excitement in too many directions. The list of action areas needs to be organized into a focused agenda. You can't accomplish everything today, but you can decide what you are able to do today—and what you want to do next quarter, next year, or even a few years down the line.

In most organizations, employees have little extra time. So be kind to yourself and to your fellow network members and don't take on more than you can handle. Recognize you don't have time for everything and choose those activities that best support members.

> One of the things that we came to grips with was the idea we are volunteers. There are a limited number of people who are going to put in a lot of high energy to get the thing done. So we just said out loud a lot, "It's OK to go slow."
>
> —*Women's network leader*

The key to a network's success, especially in the first few years, is to make sure that you are doing the following three things with your activities:

- Responding to what network members want
- Reinforcing the bottom-line benefits of the network
- Making a positive contribution to the organization

Where Are the Members?

But first of all, who are these members? So far we've only discussed the core group of women's network initiators. How do you get from those six to ten or twenty people to a companywide organization? The simplest, most straightforward way is to send out an announcement. If it can come from the CEO, that would be wonderful. If you've assembled a group of senior leaders who agree on the value of establishing a women's network, so much the better—the announcement could go out over their names. If nothing else, the core group can make the announcement itself. In any case the announcement should be an invitation to participate in the network, at a choice of levels. It should include a description of what the network is and then give options that invitees can choose from, such as

- Put my name on your mailing list.
- I want to be an active member of the network.
- Let me know how I can join the leadership team.

The announcement should include the date and time of the first full-fledged network meeting.

But there's work to do before that first public announcement. One of the first decisions you need to make as a network is on the criteria for membership. Will you include all women in the organization, or only women in certain functions or levels? Will you focus on specific locations or divisions or have a national network? What about men? Deciding membership eligibility can be difficult, but it is obviously essential. Once made, the decision also helps clarify the network's purpose.

Inclusive and exclusive membership each offer their own rewards and drawbacks. Usually, a network with an inclusive membership will have more support and be able to reach out to a wider audience. Many women's networks decide on a philosophy of including all women in the organization because not doing so reinforces the lack of access the network was formed to address.

However, reaching out to all women in an organization requires significantly more work on the part of leaders and members. There needs to be a wider range of activities—to respond to the more diverse needs of members—and a stronger communications link to reach people who don't otherwise have occasion to talk or write to each other. Particularly while the network is getting started, it takes a

good deal more effort to maintain internal systems and membership when anyone can join than when there's a narrow focus.

If you are not making the network all-inclusive, you might divide your workforce up by level, location, function, or gender—or any mix of these lines.

Level

This is most often the trickiest and most important of membership questions.
Increasingly, women's networks are started by middle- and senior-level women
and thus tend to focus on the issues facing women at those levels. Networks with
limited membership are sometimes subject to backlash from other women.

> Our original charter stated that we wanted to support women who were aspir-
> ing to management or were already in management positions. Well, that imme-
> diately alienated every secretary in the company and they started a
> tremendously negative PR wave . . . it was quite well organized and really neg-
> ative. And so, a whole wave of women had absolutely no interest in having any-
> thing to do with us.
>
> —*Women's network leader*

Some women's networks, however, would find less senior-level support if they
did include all women. These networks are successful because the members are all
familiar to senior management. Too general a representation of women, some
report, can also lead to an unfocused agenda and dilute the impact of the network.

> If the purpose of the group is just to network, then it's fine to include women
> at all levels. But if the purpose of the group is to advise the corporation, to
> make really positive concrete changes within the corporation, then I have some
> real questions about whether all-levels gives the group the credibility that is
> needed.
>
> —*Women's network leader*

> One of the problems that we have found in groups that have tried to be all
> things to everybody is, are they really anything to anyone? And I find it amus-
> ing how much management liked the idea of it being for everybody. It's safe.
> But you're not going to get anything done.
>
> —*Women's network leader*

In considering the levels of women to include, recognize that networks with
a wider membership group offer many women in the company a bonus: *Mid-level*

and junior women gain critical developmental opportunities through their involvement with the network and their work on teams. That, in turn, better prepares them for future leadership roles within the network and takes pressure off more senior women.

> It's been a really great experience to watch our lowest-level women take on committees. We've had secretaries and analysts grab a committee and some of them have been the most productive committees. They've grown in their skills by having to chair groups.
>
> *—Women's network leader*

Location

When women's networks first started, Catalyst called them "corporate women's groups" because they were almost exclusively at the corporate headquarters. Women's networks now reach across locations and, in some cases, around the globe. The decision to include women from all locations or to focus on one office or region is one that has logistical implications for the network's leadership and activities.

As with the other membership questions, the more locations you include, the more energy the network will require. Linking regions into a network, creating activities reflecting those regional members' needs, and ensuring that the activities are consistent across locations can be a great deal of work. Catalyst often recommends that new networks think small when it comes to geography. Even in

---

It's a Trade-Off

Including all women requires . . .

- Activities that address the needs of all members—either a larger number of activities, or activities that reach out to a larger group of members
- A leadership team reflective of the levels represented in the membership
- Strong communications tools such as specialized newsletters or e-mail messages to reach all members

Including only certain levels of women requires . . .

- Clear strategies to address the concerns of women not included
- Activities with a positive ripple effect on the rest of the women in the organization
- A strong rationale for the membership decision, with an understanding of the positive and negative impact on the network

Beyond Corporate Employees—McDonald's

Many organizations have women in such independent roles as franchisees or brokers. These women work independently and may feel isolated. They often need networks even more than others, and there's no reason why they shouldn't have them. For example, a new kind of network was born when the chairman of McDonald's Corporation decided the company wasn't using the talents of women franchise owners to the fullest extent. He brought ten women owners together as a task force to look at the environment for their peers.

As a result, the Women Operators Network (WON) was founded in 1988. WON's board includes representative women franchise owners, all of whom help others in their particular regions. If a woman is having a difficult situation in her store, board members may actually appear on the scene to help out. That way they get to know each other while they provide support. Other activities include a bimonthly newsletter and an annual conference on how to run better restaurants. The network's major accomplishment has been getting McDonald's Spouse Certification Program off the ground. Designed to ensure that spouses (wives in particular) of franchisees qualify for operator status, the program has resulted in a 300 percent increase in female franchisees; McDonald's has the highest number of female-owned franchises in the country.

companies that have advanced telecommunications technology, it can be difficult to keep up with a widely decentralized membership—and getting together for a face-to-face meeting poses real problems.

Many networks approach geographic expansion in phases—they may start in one or two locations, then gradually bring in more. That way, they can deal with the expected challenges on a smaller scale at first. Established women's networks often include as many as fifteen or twenty locations.

The actual structure of a network in more than one location varies. You can have one network that includes women from many locations. Or you can have many subgroups—all led by the same steering team and guiding principles and with the same name, but each with different focuses and activities.

Function

Of late, many women's networks target women in a certain field, such as operations or marketing. This allows the groups to concentrate on the specific barriers and opportunities for women in that field. This approach works well in organizations where employees are naturally grouped by function, either because of the unique culture of the specialty or because of geographic separation.

If you're thinking of creating a network focusing exclusively on the needs of women in a certain function, be careful not to isolate yourself from the rest of the organization. It's a good idea to check for other related efforts within the company and link up with them. While you may have a limited agenda, you can get a good deal of support from the rest of the company if you look for it—and your efforts will inevitably have an impact on those of others whether you consider them or not, so it's best to think things through and avoid negative side effects.

Gender

> We have a couple of people on our women's council steering committee this year saying that we should admit men into the general membership, and that we should look at men's and women's issues. Others are saying "Our mission says it is for women and if men want to support that mission, that's wonderful. If men need to have their issues addressed, they can go form a men's council."
>
> —*Women's network leader*

If it's a women's network, why should men be included? That's a good question, and one that many women's networks are asking themselves. Historically, women's networks have been just that—for the women and of the women. A few men have participated in an activity here and there, but they haven't been formally included.

However, in the last ten years, more of the issues addressed by women's networks have come to affect both men and women. For example, now that 60 percent of all married couples are dual-career couples, more men need strategies to balance their home and work lives. Catalyst's 1998 study of dual-career couples, *Two Careers, One Marriage,* showed that both spouses in dual-career marriages tend to want the same benefits at work (flexible hours being the top choice). Women's networks have realized that, and have started to include men in work/life committees.

The increased involvement of men stems both from these shared concerns and from the need for a broader base of support. Women's networks can't survive without the support of men in the organization. A network can include men in activities or it can involve them more fundamentally by including them as members. Inviting men to join pulls their perspective, both its positive and its negative aspects, into the group.

Most groups that include men as members still have "women-only" activities. In most cases, the support-related activities are primarily attended by women. It's important to continue the woman-to-woman connections that fuel the network, but reaching out to men can reenergize the network and ensure that men's opinions are represented.

Kraft Foods: Women in Operations

At Kraft, when senior leadership looked at the changing workforce in 1993, they saw that women's representation in mid-level positions at the company was fairly good except in operations. That was sort of a "last frontier" for women, especially in those areas with direct line responsibility for manufacturing and engineering, where the numbers of women were particularly low.

In 1995, three Women in Operations (WIO) teams were formed to advance women into positions of influence and exposure and to target them to lead or participate in projects critical to the organization's success. There are now twenty-two teams, with ten more in the offing for next year. With sixty-six operations sites across North America, the challenge is to connect the overall principles of WIO with local programs that are relevant to each individual group. The recent transfer of a Women's Sales Council member into operations and her joining the leadership team of WIO has forged a new alliance between those two networks. At some plants WIO and the Kraft African American Council have worked on joint initiatives.

Kraft's top leadership is extremely supportive of WIO: At the major operations facility, WIO holds a conference every other year at which the SVP of operations meets daily with employees; when planning their last conference they received a note from the EVP of Worldwide Operations and Technology for Philip Morris requesting that he be allowed to speak. The commitment of senior leaders has shown employees that it's OK to use the benefits and programs that are available. Kraft also uses WIO for testing and rolling out new initiatives, which further legitimizes the group's role in the corporation. In the last five years, WIO has created a cultural shift at Kraft—it's become apparent that, as gender demographics changed in operations, business results improved.

Creating a Mission Statement

Our mission is a business-focused one. It says we want to increase the effectiveness and status of women in support of the company's business strategies. In addition to that mission, we have three objectives. They are "upward mobility," "training and development," and "mentoring and networking." Each objective then has an operating subcommittee devoted to it.

—*Women's network leader*

The mission statement needs to be broad but still clearly outline the purpose and the overall goals of the network, and strategies to achieve those goals. It is

---

Elements of a Strong Mission Statement

- Make the business case for the network clear and explicit.
- Set the tone for the network, using company language and style.
- Use terms understood by all network audiences—members, senior leaders, managers, Human Resources, and male and female employees throughout the organization.
- Allow for flexibility in network goals and activities over time.
- Make it possible for all goals and activities to link back to the mission statement.

---

written to guide the network, but is also the simplest and clearest way to introduce the network to its diverse audiences. Crafting this mission statement is an exercise in clarification—clarifying for yourselves, for new and potential members, and for the organization the why and how of the network. Once you have a statement that really lays out your purpose and goals, planning—that is, making choices among the dizzying array of possible programs and activities that beckon to a new network—becomes much easier.

> We developed a three-year strategic plan that's based on our mission and the goals. It describes what we'll do in pursuit or in support of those goals. And it's been a wonderful thing to be able to hand to an executive . . . it really gives us some credibility. It keeps us focused and gets us support from the corporate level.
>
> —*Women's network leader*

Setting an Agenda

Once the decisions about membership and mission have been made—and not before—the new network can begin to establish an agenda. The goals, objectives, and time frames set here will provide a blueprint for everything the network does from now on.

All the lists created in earlier steps of the organizational process—the lists of member interests, company climate, network climate, needs of women, and roles of the network—provide invaluable input for the steering team. Each member of the team should try melding the lists together, then the group as a whole should spend time together creating a two- or three-year planning time frame for the network—considering what to do at all and what to do first.

In determining priorities, it's helpful to organize the different activities and needs into overarching categories. These are the most common:

- Strengthening the network
- Member networking and support
- Career development
- Advising management and human resources
- Community outreach
- High-visibility activities

As you look over the list of common activities for women's networks in Chart 2.1 (starting on page 38), take these hints into consideration: Especially in the beginning, select activities that achieve more than one goal—if you try to create many separate activities you can dissipate your energy on logistics and wear out your available volunteers. Also, think twice before you schedule high-visibility activities. They require a much higher level of energy and time on the part of members.

Finally, be sure to attach a realistic time frame to each of the network's activities, and think about evaluation tools. For now, the end result of this work should be a summary of goals in the form of the activities you plan to set up, both short-term and long-term, with dates attached to each. See Chapter Five for a detailed guide to planning and executing the events when you are ready to do so.

Checklist

☐ Make a decision about membership eligibility—and understand its implications.

☐ Create a summary list of activities and roles.

☐ Prepare a mission statement.

☐ Gather input from people reflecting the full range of potential members and select a set of first-year goals, with time frames.

☐ Set priorities and develop a two- to three-year time frame of activities.

☐ Review goals, activities, and time frames to make sure they are realistic, achievable, and directly related to needs of members and the company.

Chart 2.1 Setting Your Agenda: Common Women's Network Activities and Their Purposes

Activity	Strengthening the Network	Member Networking and Support	Career Development	Advising Management and Human Resources	Community Outreach	High-Visibility Activity
Hold brown-bag lunches for members		✓				
Start a book club for network members to read and discuss current writing on women's issues and general career topics		✓	✓			
Set up an on-line chat room or e-mail discussion group for network members		✓				
Present awards to women who receive significant promotions at the company		✓				✓
Maintain a directory of network members, including interests and career background	✓	✓				
Hold cocktail receptions where members can network with senior women	✓	✓				
Invite female board members to speak at a network meeting	✓ (if speaker decides to join)	✓		✓		
Hold informal social events with women and senior executives, designed to increase the visibility of women	✓	✓		✓		
Meet regularly with senior executives to review network activities and gender issues	✓			✓		
Design and distribute an informational brochure about the network, summarizing purpose, bottom-line benefits, and activities	✓					✓

Chart 2.1 Continued

Activity	Strengthening the Network	Member Networking and Support	Career Development	Advising Management and Human Resources	Community Outreach	High-Visibility Activity
Publish a newsletter for the network—sent to members and posted throughout the organization	✓					✓
Write articles about the network for the company newsletter or magazine	✓					✓
Reach out to other employees interested in forming an employee network and act as their adviser	✓					
Hold an annual companywide dinner, attended by senior executives, managers, Human Resources, and network members, to publicize the network and its achievements	✓	✓		✓		✓
Design an annual network conference with career development events and inside and outside speakers	✓	✓	✓	✓	✓	✓
Hold Take Our Daughters to Work Day events						✓
Publish a calendar of women's achievements for the company, highlighting women inside and outside the organization	✓					✓
Run seminars on career development issues, such as "Strategies for Advancement" or "How to Find a Mentor"		✓	✓			
Host leadership forums highlighting career paths and strategies of senior women		✓	✓			

(continued)

Chart 2.1 Continued

Activity	Strengthening the Network	Member Networking and Support	Career Development	Advising Management and Human Resources	Community Outreach	High-Visibility Activity
Publish a directory of executives, managers, and senior women available to act as coaches or mentors for network members		✓	✓			
Organize mentoring programs for members			✓			
Run a speakers series open to all employees on current topics of interest, such as "Parenting in the '90s," "Dual-Career Issues," "Stress Management"		✓				✓
Organize speeches or seminars on hot topics for the company, such as "Globalization in Today's Business" or "The Safety Initiative and How It Relates to You"		✓	✓			✓
Publish a directory of training and developmental opportunities at the company, available to all employees			✓			✓
Design ongoing efforts to inform all employees about the various programs available to them, such as work/life balance support and career development opportunities	✓	✓	✓	✓		✓
Hold résumé workshops or career retooling events during downsizing activities						✓
Create a resource library on women's issues, including books, video tapes, outside resources, and network information				✓		

Chart 2.1 Continued

Activity	Strengthening the Network	Member Networking and Support	Career Development	Advising Management and Human Resources	Community Outreach	High-Visibility Activity
Assist Human Resources and management in gathering and analyzing data related to women's advancement at the company				✓		
Review current policies and programs in place, such as flexible work arrangements or career development systems				✓		
Conduct a benchmarking study, comparing the organization's programs and policies to competitors, companies in the region, and breakthrough organizations				✓		
Assist the company in researching potential company initiatives or programs, such as a child care center or a redesigned succession planning program				✓		
Present awards to managers at all levels who support, mentor, and advance women				✓		✓
Hold managers' forums to discuss network issues in detail and design responses at the managerial level to those issues				✓		✓
Cosponsor seminars on benefits issues with Human Resources				✓		✓
Pilot career development programs for the organization			✓	✓		
Participate in the company's diversity council	✓			✓		

(continued)

Chart 2.1 Continued

Activity	Strengthening the Network	Member Networking and Support	Career Development	Advising Management and Human Resources	Community Outreach	High-Visibility Activity
Participate in company-wide teams formed to address women's opportunities at the organization	✓			✓		
Ask the CEO to write a letter about the women's network to be included in new employee orientation materials	✓			✓		
Partner with the recruitment office to interview and follow up with female candidates the organization would like to hire				✓		
Develop a network of other women's network leaders and members in your region	✓	✓			✓	
Partner with local community to help women in your region (creating a clothing bank, volunteering at the local shelter)		✓			✓	
Hold fundraisers for local women's organizations					✓	
Reach out to women's groups in your area, such as the YWCA, and tap into their programs and activities for women		✓	✓		✓	
Partner with community high schools and colleges to support and mentor female students					✓	
Offer a scholarship for promising female students					✓	
Develop an internship program for women in high school and college to work at your company				✓	✓	

NETWORK SNAPSHOT

A BUSINESS INITIATIVE THAT REACHES BEYOND MEMBERS: TEXAS INSTRUMENTS

Origins. In 1989 Jerry Junkins, TI's then-CEO, created teams of employees at all levels and locations to look at workforce 2000 issues. As a result, an HR staffer pulled together ten people to act as founders of a women's network in the semiconductor (SC) division. (Networks at TI are called initiatives because their focus is on changing the culture of the organization.) These founding members included both women and men and reflected the racial diversity of the workforce (a quality that TI insists on). The group decided to focus on business strategies rather than networking events, since other initiatives held events that SC people could attend.

Support. An initiative subteam—one Hispanic woman, one white woman, one white man, and one black woman—took their plan to SC's senior leadership and received its full support. To build support among middle management, invitations to events come from both senior management and the network. And the initiative gives awards to managers and executives who work with the network.

Membership. The initiative is open to all employees. At the beginning, there was concern as to how colleagues and managers would view membership in a women's group. Would it have a negative effect on members' careers? The organizers decided it was critical for TI to have a network that addressed gender issues. Their mission focuses on opportunities for women, yet their "vision" (TI for mission) statement has never mentioned women; it addresses improving the environment for all employees.

Leadership. From the beginning, the group created four teams: work/life balance, career development, benchmarking, and community involvement. The teams took advantage of the TI quality improvement model to reinforce the view that the women's initiative was like any other business initiative at the company.

Major Successes. When the work/life balance team began in 1993, there were no such programs at TI semiconductor, so the team decided to conduct a survey on the subject. However, once corporate-level leaders heard about it, they decided to make the survey TI-wide. As a result of the survey, SC hired a work/life manager, began to offer a resource referral service, created a parents network, joined the American Business Collaboration for Quality Child Care, and created new-mothers' rooms.

Activities and Events. The group's first event was an open forum (any employee could attend), to share information about the network and to invite questions; the invitation came from SC's senior leadership, which made high-level support clear.

One of the newest events was Tech '97, which brought together all the technical women at TI to share information about technology and discuss women's issues. Organizers also invited women at other companies—Motorola, Lucent, MCI, and several others. About six hundred women attended.

Communications. The group always celebrates its successes. Whenever a woman is promoted, initiative members get an announcement noting the woman's involvement in the network—not only to reinforce the importance of the network to advancement but also to remove any fear that participation might hurt someone's career. In addition, the group stays in touch with the other initiatives in the many business units at TI—for African Americans, for Asians, and so on—on a monthly basis through the TI Diversity Network, sharing ideas and strategies. Members can take part in person or by phone. Those who can't make it at all still get the minutes by e-mail. There's also a diversity newsletter that goes out three to four times a year and highlights what all the networks and initiatives are doing.

CHAPTER THREE

ON YOUR MARK, GET SET:
GETTING ORGANIZED AND STARTED

Guiding Question: What's the best way to organize a network?

While you are in the organizing stage, there's one final area you need to deal with—the internal network systems. No matter how deep and heartfelt the organizers' common purpose and how well they work together by tacit agreement, taking the time at the start to create a clear leadership structure, outline members' responsibilities, and design internal communications strategies will save a lot of time later.

> When we started we were so happy to be together and so full of enthusiasm and ideas. We felt connected and we had this very democratic approach where it was total consensus. Then, after about a year and a half it fell apart. Little factions developed and we had no real structure. It was painful, but we had to talk about the fact that we weren't agreeing and we ended up asking one particular woman to chair the group, who's going to take the flack and really guide or steer things. You can't just have this totally free-wheeling body that's going to expect to go anywhere.
>
> —*Women's network leader*

Like any group or task force within an organization, a women's network needs leaders who lay out the activities of the network and members who do the work. In this section, we will review two areas: establishing a network structure and developing internal communications strategies. Doing these two things well results in a smooth-running network. Not doing these two things leads to a disorganized network without a clear message for its members. The internal structure and communications go together, and when both are strong, the network has a clear advantage in moving its agenda forward.

Putting a Structure in Place

You don't need a bureaucracy that weighs you down, but you do need a system in place that reflects the goals of the network and the interests of the members.

The most common approach for networks is to have a steering team made up of the leader of the network and the leaders of various subcommittees. Subcommittees can be *activity focused* (like the "annual conference" team); they can be *issue focused* (like the "work/life balance" team); or they can be *network focused* (like the "network-communications" team). Or they can combine all three. The steering team of ten to twenty people often gets together on a monthly or bimonthly basis to review progress, discuss emerging issues, and determine the future direction of the network. The general membership of the network, usually much larger, is made up of "active" members who participate on subteams or lead activities and "nonactive" members who attend events but don't necessarily participate in their design or roll-out.

In this section, we review various aspects of choosing good leaders and designing an appropriate structure with member involvement. As with most human endeavors, there's no one best way, so we also share the comments of women's network leaders who have practical experience with each topic.

> We started about three years ago and about a year and a half ago tried to formalize because we were very loose. So we adopted a structure where we have a chairman and a vice-chairman and a steering committee.
>
> —*Women's network leader*

> We have a Board of Directors with eleven people.
>
> —*Women's network leader*

> We have a steering committee made up of the chairs of each committee plus our diversity manager, a finance person, and a woman vice president. So, total, we have about ten people on our steering committee.
>
> —*Women's network leader*

> Our core group has a rotating chair. Somebody starts the meeting and somebody takes the minutes. Whoever takes the minutes is the next chair and some-

body else volunteers to take the minutes because everybody's busy and no one really wanted the responsibility of being chairperson—it's just too overwhelming.

—Women's network leader

Who Wants to Lead?

Being the leader of a women's network can be both an exhilarating and exhausting job. Some of her most common roles include

- Acting as spokesperson for the group within the company and externally
- Ensuring the network's activities support the outlined goals and objectives
- Maintaining momentum for the group among the members and within the company
- Coordinating the activities of the members
- Keeping Human Resources and senior management informed of the group's work
- Securing participation and increasing membership when appropriate

This can be as rewarding as it is time-consuming, because of the combination of practical skills and exposure the incumbent gains. To cite just one experience,

> We've found that the women who have been cochairs of the women's group tend to have tremendous success in their professional lives because of what they've gained by having to kind of scratch through. Because if you were the chair, you had to develop budgets and present them to the president, brief him periodically—you got the visibility from him, but you also got some real-life job skills.
>
> *—Women's network leader*

If no one has yet emerged as the natural leader of your network, look over your initial steering group for someone who is recognized as a contributor in the organization and who already has access to and credibility with senior management and Human Resources. You want someone with strong commitment to the mission and goals of the group, good understanding of group process, and strong facilitation skills. It is essential that the leader who sets the tone for the network know how to build a team and to share responsibility. The leader also needs a flexible attitude and the ability to adapt to the changing needs and challenges of the network, along with sufficient interpersonal skills to communicate effectively both within the group and to other constituencies. Many if not all of these qualifications can be developed while someone is in office—but the more the leader can bring to the job, the more smoothly things will go.

Because of the amount of work required of leaders, it's important to create a succession plan. That way, you don't end up with one woman leading the network indefinitely, a scenario that can result in burnt-out leaders and a reliance on doing things "the way they've always been done." Effective network leaders recognize the need to develop their own replacements.

I took this leadership role on when I started this group, but I never planned to be involved in it on a permanent basis, other than as a sponsor. Yet I found that I ended up having to keep pulling it all together. . . . You can't accomplish exciting programs if you don't have people behind you helping.

—*Women's network leader*

I think the real trick as the group matures is for those who are leaders to inspire and transfer that knowledge to the people who take over.

—*Women's network leader*

Some networks build in this succession with a rotating leadership system or by sharing the responsibilities among two or three women. It's critical to define term lengths for leaders, overlap experienced leaders with newly elected leaders, and fill up the pipeline with interested, active members as future leaders of the network.

We have two coordinators. Their terms run for two years and there's one elected each year to make sure there's someone with experience training the less experienced coordinator.

—*Women's network leader*

Our steering committee has a three-year term, with one-third changing each year.

—*Women's network leader*

We have a three-year max for the time you can serve on the steering committee, so we're constantly flowing new people in. We have a post-chair, a pre-chair, and a current chair.

—*Women's network leader*

Those of us on the board try to look and see who could come up behind us to fill committee chairs over time.

—*Women's network leader*

Who's Doing the Work?

> We have a program committee where we put together our monthly programs. We have a marketing committee that does our publications and our newsletters. We have our issue committee, where women can get together and talk about their own issues and share information on an informal basis.
>
> —*Women's network leader*

> We form subcommittees for various things as needed and then dissolve them if we don't need them anymore.
>
> —*Women's network leader*

> We have four committees—-nominating, communications, events, and finance. We have a special group on career development and training which has been fairly active in getting information out.
>
> —*Women's network leader*

Committees are the centers of action in women's networks. There are four distinct kinds.

Activity-focused committees exist to put in place a certain program or event and are usually made up of members who are interested in the topic or have a particular expertise in the area. Committees in this category might organize a speakers series, set up a networking breakfast, or design and implement a network mentoring program. They often have a shorter life than other committees, organizing the event and disbanding once it's over. The key to success for them is enough staff to plan and execute the event and access to the required resources (Human Resources, financial support, or whatever they need to get the job done).

Issue-focused committees, such as those on career development or work/life balance, exist to examine longer-term issues related to women's advancement. These groups might design appropriate solutions to the challenges women face in the organization or make recommendations to management and Human Resources. They can continue for a number of years, with a different focus each year. For example, a career development subteam can focus on mentoring one year and develop a pilot mentoring program for the network. The next year, the same team might focus on performance review systems. Its work that year could include benchmarking the company's review processes against other companies and coming up with recommendations to senior management and Human Resources.

Because these issues are so large, it can often seem that the group is making little progress. To overcome this appearance, successful issue-focused committees set up focused agendas, with the goal of a clear outcome at the end of each year.

Network-focused committees exist to oversee the internal systems of the network. These teams often focus on communications, membership, marketing, finance, or nominating new slates of leaders. They exist for the life of the network; members often rotate on and off. Some members will find service on such committees less interesting—less of a change from everyday work—than service on the other types of committees, so the network should limit the number of committees in this category and make an effort to keep the rotation flowing smoothly.

A new trend has emerged in network committees because of the intense time constraints of many network members. Committees have a shorter tenure and only exist if enough members are interested in the topic. This more fluid and time-conscious approach ensures that the network focuses only on issues and activities of interest to members and sustainable by the network.

> If you want to see an idea happen, bring a proposal to a meeting, make sure it connects to the mission, tell us what you need to do it, pitch it to the people there, see if you can get support, and go for it.
>
> *—Women's network leader*

A final piece of advice. Whatever the structure, network leaders should stress the importance of developing work plans for each committee. These should include the appropriate network objective, time frame, necessary resources, and evaluation measurements. When these activities are formalized, network leaders have a clear sense of what each subteam is working on—and team members have a better understanding of their own roles and responsibilities.

> We do monthly reports, and periodically we do formal progress reports. It's all very visible and we have the opportunity to question each other and push a little if one committee is not working at a pace that is supportive of the work that other committees are doing.
>
> *—Women's network leader*

> We have a three-year strategic plan. Throughout the year all of the committees report on how they are progressing in terms of the strategic plan, where they are in terms of the things that have been set out for them to accomplish during that year, and any ad hoc committees or task teams that have come up.
>
> *—Women's network leader*

Communications Strategies

Communication within the network is often overlooked in the rush to communicate externally, but to maintain the network's momentum, it's critical to keep members aware of, involved with, and supportive of the network's direction and activities. Here is a sampling of the range of different tools networks use to keep members in the loop:

- Newsletters (quarterly or biannual)
- E-mail updates
- Computer bulletin boards
- Online chat rooms
- E-mail discussion groups
- Calendar of events and network activities
- Formal network meetings with status reports from committees
- Informal update events, such as "Hour with the President"
- Videoconferencing
- Tapes of events or meetings circulated to members
- Regularly scheduled conference call updates

The following sections discuss several tools for network development. Catalyst has found that new networks in particular can profit from this advice.

Provide Background on the Network and Why It's Here

In addition to making sure members know about meetings, events, and new developments, you also want to communicate basic information about how the network works—meeting times, structure, membership, and so on. Make sure people can find out why and how the network was formed and what the group's vision was at the beginning (and is now), as well. It's useful to assemble an introduction folder that outlines this information for all interested parties.

> We put out a calendar every month and put it on the bulletin board and it's just like a schedule of events.
>
> *—Women's network leader*

> On our memos announcing our events—we would have a statement on every one of them that everyone is welcome, and we started making it clear that men

and women were welcome. We tell people, just pass this on to anybody you think would be interested and if they want to be on the mailing list, let us know.

—*Women's network leader*

Develop a Feedback Mechanism

It pays off for a long-term network to devote a great deal of energy to understanding its membership. Without a way of getting feedback, network leadership can become isolated from the interests and needs of members. The most common strategies are annual or biannual surveys of the entire membership, short surveys handed out at the end of events, or individual conversations with selected members.

You need to both understand how the larger active and nonactive membership feels about the network's direction and to gauge the impact of specific types of activities and of the network itself. By including specific questions about how members have benefited from their participation in the network, leaders can quantify the positive impact of the network on the members and the company.

Celebrate Your Successes

Like most task forces, networks tend to spend a lot of time doing and not much time stopping and congratulating. It's important to take time each year to highlight all the network's accomplishments. After all, you've all worked hard and deserve some time to pat yourselves on the back. Some networks have a celebratory lunch. Others go so far as to have an annual conference or dinner where they formally review the year's achievements—and they're sure to invite senior leaders, Human Resources professionals, and middle managers so that they too can learn of the network's success.

Our first year, we listed the milestones; we listed what we did at every meeting and who led and so on.

—*Women's network leader*

What's In a Name?

Names mean a lot. While this may not be the most critical decision you make as a network, it's still an important one. After all, as soon as people hear there's a women's network, they'll start talking about it. It's up to you to make sure they're saying what you want them to say. You can do that through a name that reflects the group's approach and purpose and a mission statement that gives them the language you want them to use.

We used to be called Women in Power and our acronym was WIP. But we got so much guff that we changed it to Women and Men in Power, and even that made a difference.

—Women's network leader

Our group is called BWI, which stands for Business Women INC. The INC is an acronym for information and issue identification, networking, and commitment to development. We're a very acronym-oriented company. We built a mission statement and by-laws around the INC.

—Women's network leader

Our group is called the Global Partnership Network for Women. The word global is used at Bankers Trust and the women were very conscious of keeping this group as close to the business bottom-line orientation as possible. That was worth maybe four meetings.

—Women's network leader

One Last Note

As with any team or working group, it takes time for the network to mesh and function at its highest level. Don't be frustrated if there are difficult internal dynamics or if you have to take some time now and then to stop and reassess where you're going. All that time and effort makes the network stronger. It can be difficult as a leader of a network and as a member to balance the commitment required for the network against the demands of everyday work and personal life. However, as the network continues to grow and flourish, so does the commitment of the members to the group—and the benefits reaped by those same members.

There definitely has to be a strong commitment and somehow you grow that. We found that we really had to build up a level of trust where people could relax and be themselves. It takes a while to develop that.

—Women's network leader

We had a lot of women in the group who were impatient. A lot of Type A's who wanted very much to go and who were very outcome-driven. It really was a learning process for all of us to step back and say "Wait a minute here, we have to take some time to form ourselves as a group."

—Women's network leader

Checklist

☐ Create an organizational structure that uses the time and resources of the membership efficiently.

☐ Choose committed, energetic leaders who can maintain group momentum.

☐ Create a process to ensure the development of new leaders.

☐ Design internal communication systems to gain input from membership on group goals and activities.

NETWORK SNAPSHOT

AN OASIS IN FINANCIAL SERVICES: DAIN RAUSCHER

Origins. Dain Rauscher is a full-service investment services and investment banking firm with sixty-eight offices in eighteen states. When their network was founded in 1991, women in sales felt isolated in large territories in a field dominated by men, and many women felt a need for training and mentoring in how to win clients' trust and gather assets. Women, on average, made up just 9 percent of brokers. At the first meeting of the network, "to walk in and see people just like me was phenomenal," said one woman. "It felt like I had come home."

Support. The association reports to the firm's president and CEO, with an annual performance report and monthly conference calls with the CEO. The firm's top officers and other senior women executives usually attend the annual confer-

ence. According to one member, "All of the managers and regional offices support the association. They too would like to recruit and retain more female brokers and the association helps them do that."

Membership. All the firm's female brokers and many trainees are members of the association. Women are admitted after their second year at the firm, one year before they graduate from broker-trainee to broker.

Leadership. The group has a rotating board, with representatives from every region. The board reports directly to the Dain Rauscher executive committee.

Successes. The firm's recruitment and retention rate has gone up for women. Two female members of the association have been promoted to the leadership position of managers. Until the association formed, women said, it hadn't occurred to them that they could attain that title. The firm is now actively recruiting women as interns and as experienced brokers. During the network's first three years, the number of women brokers rose from forty-four to eighty-nine.

Activities and Programs. The centerpiece of the association is its annual conference, for which the firm's female brokers vote on program topics, serve on a program development committee, and organize their own two-day event, which is heavily subsidized by the firm.

Communications. The group's communications committee prepares an annual directory, a member newsletter, and recruitment materials, and also facilitates an informal phone network for members in time of need, from failing to meet sales targets to being diagnosed with breast cancer.

PART TWO

IT'S UP AND RUNNING, NOW WHAT?

Once the women's network is off the ground and word of its impending presence—if not of its here-and-now existence—is beginning to circulate, it's tempting to stop and take a breather. But there is still a great deal to do to make the network a real presence in the ongoing life of the company. The last four chapters of this guidebook cover the types of activities involved in bringing a new network to full effectiveness and managing it throughout the rest of its life span.

Chapter Four: Want Real Power? The people who first get together to form a network can do very little to move their organization on their own. To get anything substantial done, they need to establish credibility with the different constituencies in the company and build support for the network among them. This chapter shows you how to focus on ways the network stands to benefit the organization from the point of view of each constituency, so that people at all levels will recognize that it's in their own interest to accept the network and its activities.

Chapter Five: You've Arrived! By planning and executing the right network activities—events that will not only bring women employees together and help them advance in the company but that will also bring incremental benefits to the company at large—network organizers can cement their group's place in the company. This chapter discusses the types of action plans that are most effective, and also describes ways to move toward what is sometimes considered the ultimate goal of a women's network—advising management and Human Resources.

Chapter Six: Stay Focused! After the first bloom and momentum wear off a network, the amount of effort involved sometimes begins to seem overwhelming. Nonetheless, it is possible to handle the day-to-day operations of a network smoothly and efficiently, and to maintain an active and productive presence year after year. This chapter addresses some of the most common questions Catalyst receives on the subject, and discusses ways to thrive and prosper in the face of the minor setbacks any network is likely to encounter along the way.

Chapter Seven: What If You Face Real Problems? Sometimes events force a network to rethink its whole place in the company. Member needs change, company policy or ownership changes, the business climate changes. This chapter discusses ways to recognize such transitions when they begin to take shape, and to guide a network through them to ongoing success or graceful and productive dissolution.

CHAPTER FOUR

WANT REAL POWER?
BUILD COMPANYWIDE SUPPORT

Guiding Question: How can the network effectively build support and credibility among the different constituencies in the organization?

Once the network's core group has developed a presence in the organization, it needs to focus directly on gaining the support of managers, senior managers, Human Resources, and men and women throughout the company—all the specific groups necessary for the success of the network.

This means it's critical to highlight the ways the network benefits the organization. If you can do that well, then most of your job is done.

> Our approach for establishing credibility with senior management has been to be very conscious of keeping this as close to the business bottom-line orientation as humanly possible.
>
> —*Women's network leader*

The climate survey described in Chapter One helps develop the business case for the network at the broadest levels. It explores demographic trends, internal company statistics, and the specific issues facing women in the organization. The initial stages of organizing the network center on the network's role in addressing the larger organizational issues related to gender. Once all that is done, it's time to target the more specific ways the network can help groups within the company. By letting those groups know what the network can do, network organizers can begin building support almost effortlessly.

It is here that the network's communications strategies take on heightened importance. Once you understand how the network can help the company, it's critical to communicate that clearly and explicitly, addressing the specific issues of each group and making your case to audiences at all levels within the organization.

Communication comes in all shapes and sizes. Such informal strategies as individual meetings, one-to-one updates, and social events are just as crucial as formal communication vehicles like newsletters, updates, or presentations.

A brand-new network needs to build support within several major constituency groups:

- Senior management
- Middle management
- Human Resources
- Other network audiences
  Other employee networks
  Diversity councils
  Employees throughout the organization
  Men in the company
  Women not involved in the network

Each of these audiences provides critical support, but the first three are a high priority; essential to the initial success—or even the existence—of the network. The "other network audiences" are important groups, but you can focus on them after the network has been around for a while—say, after the first year.

So start with the first and most important three groups and focus on the support you have to begin with—and how to leverage it. As you design strategies to build support, there are three key questions:

1. *What support does the network currently have among these groups?*
2. *How will these levels of support affect the network activities?*
3. *What can the network do to increase that level of support?*

Catalyst has found that the most effective strategy is to build support within senior management ranks early. Top-level champions help build support among middle management simply by making their attitudes known, over and above the very real direct assistance they can give you. Trying to gain middle-level support without executive support is much more difficult. And mid-management support is critical to a network's success.

The initial work outlined in the first three chapters will probably give most network organizers a fairly good sense of the way various groups currently react to the idea of the network. Nonetheless, it's generally useful to go through the three "Support Continuum" charts presented later in this chapter, comparing the observations there to real-world findings, so as to codify and rationalize those instinctive impressions. The charts will help address whatever level of support the network currently enjoys (or faces), with a view toward moving the organization toward the high-support end of the continuum. The goal is to give you the options and tools to understand the support the network currently has in the organization, create approaches to build on that support, and develop opportunities to leverage support into action.

Senior Management

> Support from management is essential. I don't think you could have an effective group without it.
>
> *—Women's network leader*

Ideally, you'd like to have the executives in the organization applauding the group's efforts and supporting the network in any way they can. Realistically though, support from senior management varies widely. Chart 4.1 illustrates the range of what you may have to deal with. Some networks are lucky enough to start at the behest of the CEO, who then serves as a very visible champion. Other networks have to work carefully and slowly over a number of years to build that level of support. Whatever stage you're at, the support of senior management is worth working for.

In addition to listing the characteristics of various levels of support, Chart 4.1 also outlines what senior leaders and women's networks can expect from each other. After all, the best relationships are partnerships where one group helps the other. Finally, the chart outlines some options to consider as you try to increase support or build upon the support you have.

Specific Strategies to Build the Relationship with Senior Leaders

Meet Individually. This strategy allows you to reach out and build one-to-one relationships with executives. First, think about each executive separately and consider which network member should make the approach. Often this has to do with who the executive knows best or who can establish the most rapport with that leader. Next, clarify in your own mind what you want to get out of the meeting.

Chart 4.1 Support Continuum: Senior Management

High Level of Support: Championing	Medium Level of Support: Acceptance and Interest	Low Level of Support: Indifference or Opposition
Characteristics of Relationship:		
• All networks aspire to this level. It can catapult a network into a very strong and effective role, making it easy to gather data on issues, formulate recommendations, and present them to management. • Networks with this level of support can have a strong and very visible presence within the company.	• This is the most common level of support networks have from senior leadership. It includes relationships with sympathetic senior leaders, but few signs of formal support from top management as a whole. • Often, senior executives understand the purpose and benefits of the network, but gender issues are not a major priority for them. • There is less of an opportunity to advise management, but there are still opportunities to work with Human Resources or individual leaders to address women's issues.	• This is a tough spot for a network to be in, but not an impossible position. Few executives will actively discourage a women's network, but it's difficult to build support in other areas without basic support from the top.
What They Want from the Network:		
• Leaders want help in designing and implementing strategies related to women. Networks can help identify the needs of women as well as acting as a liaison between women and management.	• Often, at this level senior executives may not know enough about the network to work directly with it. They address the relevant issues via Human Resources. • Leaders need more information about the impact of the network and how it can help the organization.	• Management has few expectations.

Chart 4.1 Continued

High Level of Support: Championing	Medium Level of Support: Acceptance and Interest	Low Level of Support: Indifference or Opposition
What the Network Can Expect from Senior Management:		
• In addition to more attention for your recommendations, senior management will provide financial support, informal championing, visible role in supporting network (participation in events, and so on), regular meetings to discuss issues, and an assigned management liaison.	• Networks receive some financial support, can meet regularly as a group, and can attain a relatively high level of visibility within the organization. • There may be an informal management liaison, for advice and guidance.	• Even at this level of support, networks often carry out visible activities and events. But in some environments the lack of support at the top is mirrored throughout the organization. In these cases, it may be better to avoid high-visibility events, which may generate backlash.
Options and Strategies:		
• Leverage the support you have without overstepping your bounds. Consider your areas of focus and how senior leaders can help you achieve your goals. • Ask senior leaders to assist you in building relationships with others. • If you are focusing on programmatic activities, such as events or speakers, senior leaders can give speeches or write letters to potential audience members. • You may be in a position to work with management directly, advising them on approaches related to women's advancement.	• Communication is especially critical at this point. If you can successfully make the case for the network, then you may be able to gain a higher level of support. • Presentations to senior managers or individual meetings with leaders are effective. Focus on their needs that the network could meet, reinforce the partnership with management, and outline the bottom-line benefits of the network. • Be realistic about what you need from senior executives. As you start to gain support, carve out small and easy roles for leaders and then build to more active and visible responsibilities.	• Examine what is preventing senior leaders from supporting you. Do they not understand the purpose of the network? Are they concerned about how far the network wants to go? Do they think gender is not an issue at the organization? Design an approach based on that information. • The strategy of working with senior leaders one by one works best here. A champion within management can help pave the way with others, and offer you advice on how to approach them.

Some common goals:

- *Providing an introduction to the network*—its mission, goals, and strategies.
- *Presenting the business case for the network's existence*—why it's needed and how it will help the organization.
- *Understanding the leader's concerns about the network*—is there a real need for it? Is it likely to have negative results?
- *Answering individual concerns and reinforcing the importance of the network and how it will directly help the leader*—position support of the network as benefiting the individual you're talking to as well as benefiting the network.
- *Explaining what you'd like from the leader*—a champion role, help in placing the network on meeting agendas, informal advice, attendance at major network events, and so on.

Dos and Don'ts of Advising Management: How to Get Your Feet Wet Without Getting in Over Your Head

In the last few years, women's networks have increasingly been asked to become involved in the design and implementation of strategies related to women's advancement. The *good news* is that this trend indicates an increased emphasis and interest by corporations on these issues as well as the increased credibility of women's networks within the organization. The *bad news* is that most women's networks lack the time, knowledge, and power to implement larger initiatives. So how does an effective network involve itself in shaping policy? The key is for everyone to be clear on where the network's role begins and ends:

Dos: It's appropriate for networks to be involved in the design of initiatives and in helping their organization's leaders understand the issues raised and the possible solutions. Successful networks can also participate in the rollout of the initiative—as advisers or troubleshooters.

Don'ts: It's less wise, however, to be seen as the *drivers* of these efforts or to allow yourself to be held accountable for their success. Those roles are better assumed by senior leadership or Human Resources. Women's networks can evaluate the impact of these efforts or pilot some of them. Networks that take on responsibility for leading such efforts often cannot achieve their goals because they lack necessary resources. So if offered the opportunity to get involved in such an initiative, be sure to take it—but also be sure to clarify roles early so you can leverage your place in the organization.

Presentations to the Leadership Team. It is also important to educate senior leadership as a group. This allows for discussion and provides visibility for the network. Many women's networks make a formal presentation to the senior management team at some point in the first year of existence.

Begin by approaching a senior leader about your interest in speaking to the group about the network. Such a presentation is most likely to become a reality if someone within the senior team suggests it. Otherwise, go to the top yourself and request some time at an upcoming meeting. You may even succeed in scheduling a meeting devoted only to network discussions.

Whatever the format, here's what to do:

1. *Reinforce the business case!* If they come away with nothing else, the leaders should have learned how and why the network will help the company's bottom line. Now is the time to make sure your business case argument is watertight. The numbers you use should be unmistakable and the logic unassailable. The more information you give to senior leaders, the more they can use that data in championing the network.

2. *Tell them what the network is and what it isn't.* Catalyst often hears that senior executives may have qualms about supporting a network because they think it is a "radical organization." Virtually all women's networks aren't—and it's your job to make that point convincingly. Explain what the group's mission and purpose is, how it was developed, and how it relates to the company's goals. The very best way to get these issues out in the open is to persuade a sympathetic member of the senior team to plant the right questions.

3. *Give them details about your upcoming activities.* By providing concrete information about scheduled events, you reinforce how the network will fulfill its mission. This can also give top execs the opportunity to offer input about those events (and for you to actively solicit it) and for them to volunteer to participate in an upcoming event.

4. *Establish a venue for ongoing communication.* Don't let it end with this first meeting. Think about other ways you can keep the leadership in the loop. Networks often set up quarterly or biannual meetings with management. Regular lunches or written updates are other ways to keep in touch with this group. A management liaison who regularly reports to leadership is also effective. Clarify that mechanism in this meeting. Be sure to take the approach commonly used in your company for business agendas, whatever it may be.

Before you go into this meeting, create a strong and detailed document outlining the benefits and positive impact of the network. It should be brief and action-oriented—something the execs can take away and mull over later. Also, think about meeting dynamics. Talk to your champions in advance and ask for their guidance. Approach individual leaders for support in terms of asking certain questions or defending you in the meeting.

No matter how much advance work is required, the benefits are enormous. Having this group in one room focusing on the network has a tremendous impact and can be an opportunity to establish an ongoing relationship with leaders.

Create Informal Opportunities for Network Members and Leaders to Meet. Sometimes formal meetings aren't the best way to go, perhaps due to organizational politics or culture. Many networks then decide to promote the network to management more informally—by selling the professionalism and commitment of the members themselves.

Social events provide a forum where members and leaders can interact. Sometimes it's an informal lunch for network leaders and selected management representatives. Other times it's a cocktail party after work. Sometimes an event during the workday is better because of time limitations after work. Other times, an event after work is less formal. Think about what venue would fit best with the culture of your organization. You want to concentrate on making members most comfortable and getting leaders' undivided attention.

Letting senior leaders meet network members at such an event can go a long way toward allaying leaders' fears about what the network might do. While this strategy requires less written work than a formal presentation, there is still plenty of advance preparation involved. Think about

- The points you want to make about the network
- The people you want to persuade to accept those points
- The best network member to make those points to each leader
- The ways network members can show themselves off to best advantage

Bonus: *The event offers the additional advantage of providing the opportunity for individual members to network with management, which is essential for personal advancement.* Recognize that this will be a result of the event and plan accordingly.

Strategies to Leverage the Relationship

Once you have achieved some senior management support, don't hesitate to make the most of it. For example, if your network has problems with membership because of supervisor resistance, you can ask a senior leader to write invitation letters to potential members and either copy that letter to their supervisors or write a separate letter to managers asking for their support. Here are some other ways for leaders to support a women's network, on a rising scale of commitment:

- Speak with leaders from other companies who are involved with their company's women's network.
- Review information on network strategies and activities.
- Meet regularly with the group to learn of activities and results.
- Include a network representative on the organization's diversity council.
- Act as a management liaison.
- Include updates and discussions regarding the network at executive meetings.
- Highlight the network and its value through company newsletters or executive updates.
- Attend network events.
- Participate in the group's kick-off event.
- Be a speaker at a group event.
- Ensure subordinates' support of the network.
- Integrate the network's recommendations into organizational policies and procedures.
- Actively work to build support for the network throughout the organization.

Management Liaison

Once you've made connections with a few leaders, consider who might act as a liaison or adviser to the network. Many women's networks have such advisers, either formally or informally. Like a mentor, a liaison assists you in developing realistic goals, building support in various parts of the organization, and guiding you through organizational land mines. This relationship is especially important if you have uneven support among management. As many network leaders point out, having a champion to push for the network during those informal management conversations really makes a difference.

Middle Management

Middle management has the most power in the organization. It doesn't matter whether your president or your vice president supports the network. The five or six on top can have all of these great ideas about diversity, but middle management is who most of us are dealing with en masse.

—Women's network leader

Obviously, opinions differ. But it's clear that a network, even if it has support from senior management, can't get along without middle management. Since these are the individuals who implement the strategies and approaches designed by the company's leadership, any network activities intended to have a broad impact on the organization must be supported by middle management.

In addition, because this group often includes the supervisors or colleagues of network members, it is difficult to develop, maintain, and expand a strong membership without their support.

> Philosophically, it's very easy for middle managers to support the network, but when it comes to that day when the woman disappears for a couple of hours, they can't handle it. That's where the problems come in. A woman says that she has to spend a few hours at the women's council and her boss will respond with, "You're doing that stuff again? Well I need you here. I need this done." That's where a lot of the resistance comes in.
>
> —*Women's network leader*

Comments like that are indirect but very effective, preventing women from becoming involved in the network. Some women report that colleagues make jokes about their work with the network or send more subtle messages that it's not a productive way to spend time. Whatever the situation is, building understanding and support among middle management early is essential to building strong membership. Chart 4.2, while laying out the facts clearly, will also help you educate middle management about the benefits of the network and reinforce their understanding of how the network can help them.

Strategies to Build the Relationship

Target specific groups of middle managers for specific outreach strategies. For example, if you are planning to focus on career development issues within a specific area, locate the ten to fifteen most visible and important middle managers and reach out to them.

Educate and Communicate. More than anyone else in the organization, middle managers are interested in how the network can help *them*. Many managers are skeptical of new initiatives or groups because they may assume, often rightly, that it means more work for them. They need to understand how the network can help them directly. A women's network can benefit middle managers by providing

- Developmental and networking opportunities for those of their direct reports who are members of the women's network
- Information on resources or external opportunities for training

Chart 4.2 Support Continuum: Middle Management

High Level of Support: Partnership	Medium Level of Support: Acceptance	Low Level of Support: Resistance
Characteristics of Relationship:		
• Middle managers are working with the network in a range of ways, from participation in events to being members of the network. • Managers who aren't actively involved in the network are supporting those women who are. • Managers highlight importance of network informally in meetings and conversations, as well as recognizing members' contributions to the network in performance reviews.	• This level of support encompasses a wide range of endorsement. At its best, this level means informal support of the network by middle managers and few challenges to their employees involved in the network. • If your network falls into this range you don't have problems with middle managers actively discouraging members or disagreeing with the network. • There are often a handful of interested middle managers who can act as supporters of the network among this group.	• This low level of support may show in reduced membership and lower attendance at events, and even in quiet resistance to implementing network-designed initiatives. • Managers may openly criticize the network, or quietly discourage employees or colleagues from joining.
What They Want from the Network:		
• Look to the network to create events or programs that directly benefit themselves or their employees. • They may or may not actively seek out ways to be involved in the network.	• Most middle managers like the idea of the network well enough in principle, but hope it won't cost them anything. As long as they don't have to actively respond to the network—by doing work or losing employee time—the network looks like a fine idea, but they're apt to come up with reasons why requests for assistance can't be met just at present.	• Managers who don't support the network want very little from it. They usually are not interested in learning about the network and do not want the group to involve them or their employees or colleagues. • Some managers are open in their disapproval of the network and may try to actively criticize the group and its efforts.

Chart 4.2 Continued

High Level of Support: Championing	Medium Level of Support: Acceptance and Interest	Low Level of Support: Indifference or Opposition
What the Network Can Expect from Middle Management:		
• Encourage membership. • Participation in network events as speakers or panelists. • Support for network initiatives. • Inclusion of network activities in job performance reviews. • "Selling" the network to skeptical colleagues.	• Managers will allow interested women to join and recognize that participation will require employees' time.	• In this case, the network should expect very little. One can only hope that middle management's disapproval is silent and doesn't act as a roadblock for the group.
Options and Strategies:		
• Use managers effectively by carefully selecting the ways to involve them. Think about the network's goals and needs and where this group can most help. • As you strategize about larger initiatives related to women, involve middle managers as a reality check for your design process.	• The key here is education. Many of these middle managers don't understand the network's purpose and benefits. You have a good chance of increasing their support and involvement if you can show how the network helps them directly. • Because this group is so large, one-to-one meetings are less effective. However, if there are key leaders among this group, try to enlist their support. • If you're fortunate enough to have strong support from one or more senior management champions, enlist their aid with individual middle managers who oppose the network or in addressing divisional or functional meetings in areas with low support.	• Education is equally important to develop support. Focus on how the network benefits them and try to build support among individuals or pockets of managers. Ideally that support will spread. • As with the middle level of support, senior champions can be very effective in reinforcing the company's support of the network. Divisional or functional meetings where middle managers are in attendance are good opportunities to send that message. Other more formal vehicles like company newsletters or direct letters can also be effective.

Chart 4.2 Continued

High Level of Support: Championing	Medium Level of Support: Acceptance and Interest	Low Level of Support: Indifference or Opposition
Options and Strategies (continued):		
	• It is at this level that senior-level support can be effectively leveraged. The more you can show that leaders support the network, the more likely it will be that middle managers join in that support.	• Publicize network successes that benefited middle managers in company newsletters if you can gain access to them, or in direct publications or letters of your own.

- Access to information on issues such as flexibility options, career development issues, and so on
- Speakers on topics relevant to individual managers' work
- Assistance with résumés and skills identification during transitional periods
- Informal mentoring and role models for their employees

You can use a variety of vehicles to communicate those benefits. Small managerial meetings or annual "get to know the network" workshops can be effective opportunities. Some networks ask that each member inform her department of the network activities. More formal options include placing articles in the company newsletter, distributing the women's network newsletter to middle managers, or displaying posters advertising the network's mission and activities in high-traffic areas.

We use in-house communication vehicles to publish our accomplishments. We get some involvement from the executive liaison so it's not just the group saying what we did but a person of visibility and power acknowledging it and recognizing it.

—Women's network leader

From the Top Down. Nothing is more effective at persuading middle management than strong support from the top. Be sure to communicate that support clearly if you have it.

We have a very strong commitment from the top level of the organization for the women's council. So, when someone is going to serve on the steering committee, a letter goes out from the COO saying that this person is going to be involved and I strongly encourage you to support her efforts.

—Women's network leader

Successful women's networks ask that executives weave their support of the network into all the myriad interactions they have with middle managers—speeches they give, conversations they have in the hallway, letters they write to managers, and so on. Some networks specifically invite middle managers to events at which the CEO or other executives will be speaking. In this way, a strong message is sent to middle management that not supporting the network means going against what the leadership expects.

Strategies to Leverage the Relationship

There are two important ways middle managers can support the network: *assisting the group in its efforts to promote women's opportunities* and *encouraging current and potential members.* To help them help, include these managers in discussions of strategy when you're designing approaches for initiatives such as career development, flexibility, or women's advancement. Middle managers can provide important insights and ideas that will help you design effective and long-lasting strategies. You may decide to include two or three key middle managers on a task force or to consciously reach out to a larger group.

Encouraging new members requires little direct effort on the part of the managers, but they do need to allow the individuals to take time for network activities and they need to understand the benefits of participation. Some networks are very explicit:

When a new member is recruited and accepted into the network we ask that the commitment form be signed by the woman's supervisor. It clearly states what the time commitment will be and that they approve of this and will allow them that on-the-job time to do it. Hopefully there's dialogue between that woman and her supervisor when she gets accepted.

—Women's network leader

Bonus: *Some managers report that having their direct reports work in the women's network actually helps them identify developmental opportunities.* Ideally, these opportunities are then woven back into the employee's performance reviews.

With regard to participating on the women's council, one woman's boss told her, "That's great. I don't have anything I can offer you right now so if you can get some other leadership experience and broaden your horizons a little bit by doing that, then go for it."

—Women's network leader

It was actually my manager's initiative [that I get involved]. He said that I was doing a good job, but now I needed to learn the organization and broaden my networking within the company. This seemed like an easy way to do it.

—Women's network leader

The women's network offers real benefits to middle managers. As a result, making them aware of the positive impact of the network on their own work lives and responsibilities is the best strategy to gain their support.

Human Resources

Human Resources can play a strong role in supporting the network's goals and mission. The reverse is also true: if Human Resources doesn't support you, it's more difficult to achieve those goals. At its best, the relationship is a true partnership, with the women's network advising Human Resources as that department implements network recommendations. When you work with HR staff, be sure to highlight the benefits to them—for example, the joint effort may gain new support from management for long-term HR goals. Following are just some of the ways Human Resources can be your best resource:

- As you build the business case, HR can provide you with company data.
- As you are identifying the needs of women in the organization, HR can summarize employee survey responses from women.
- As you are designing a career development seminar, HR can provide you with financial resources.
- As you investigate flexibility options, HR can guide the development of a program or initiative.
- As you pilot a mentoring program, HR can assume long-term responsibility.

On the HR issue . . . we tell them we want to work with them and we certainly do. We keep asking them, "What can we do to help you accomplish the goal that you set up for the corporation?" At the same time, though, we don't want to be their buddies because we want to be able to push them. How do you keep them close to you, yet still a distance away?

—Women's network leader

There's a real symbiotic relationship between the network and Human Resources. Networks can support diversity initiatives and can provide the muscle for that person to push through their agenda. But, on the other hand, it's seen as a Human Resources program. So that takes away some of the credibility the women's network has. It's an interesting dilemma. HR really benefits from the group as well as the group benefiting from HR. Yet, there's something lost in the process.

—Women's network leader

Positioning what the network wants to accomplish is also important. Remember, by recommending a strategy, the network may be implicitly highlighting what Human Resources *isn't* doing. Consider the language you use in making suggestions, and the way you present them, to ensure you're focusing on the positive opportunities, rather than the lack of current programs.

Defining the Lines: When Network Members Are Human Resources Professionals

One factor that further complicates this relationship is the number of women in the network who work in Human Resources. In a network with a strong relationship with Human Resources, these individuals act as critical links between the two groups. In networks with less support, these women often end up feeling the need to defend Human Resources and its decisions.

Additionally, senior leaders in the company often turn first to the network member from Human Resources when discussing initiatives rather than to the formal heads of the network.

It's odd to be a member of the advisory group who has corporate Human Resources responsibility. Nine times out of ten when an issue is raised, the president will turn to me and say, "Well?"

—Women's network leader

Network members who are in Human Resources often need to make their role explicit in meetings, clarifying whether they are speaking as a network member or as a Human Resources professional, to ensure their viewpoint is understood.

The support you can gain from Human Resources is delineated tangibly and explicitly in Chart 4.3, as is the assistance networks can give to Human Resources. A strong relationship can help fuel the engine of the women's network and give it the resources required to be effective.

Strategies to Build the Relationship

If you choose individual meetings with HR staffers as an approach, many of the tips used for senior management meetings apply. There are some other strategies that are especially useful for working with HR, however.

Understand Where the Network Ends and Human Resources Begins. We can't stress this enough. Earlier, we discussed that the network needs to understand where its advising role ends and senior management's leadership role begins. Similarly, you need to be crystal clear about where your role of identifying issues and solutions ends and where HR's implementation role begins. Sometimes this means forgoing certain activities because they rightfully belong to the HR function.

> People had strong feelings that it wasn't right for us to set up a shadow government and push the whole issue of diversity. It was felt that it should properly belong to the company and that it should be promoted through standard Human Resources channels. There was such a strong feeling about not pursuing this item that belonged to HR that we chose to focus on other areas.
>
> —*Women's network leader*

Meet Regularly with Human Resources. Ease of communication is one of the most important success factors in the relationship between HR and the women's network. It is critical to inform HR of your mission, how your activities are fulfilling that mission, and the impact of those activities. Quarterly or biannual meetings with HR leadership often offer the best way to make that work. Potential overlap can be identified and each group can understand the other's interests. HR may have resources that can assist you or knowledge about a topic that can be useful to you.

> We just started meeting on a quarterly basis with our network leaders and the Vice President of Diversity and Human Resources who supported all of the networks. We meet with him and it's really helped out as far as discussing issues goes, reporting in on what the networks are doing, and applauding what they've done. It is just a feeling of motivation and it seems that since we've been doing that all of our networks have been a lot more active.
>
> —*Women's network leader*

Chart 4.3 Support Continuum: Human Resources

High Level of Support: Partnership	Medium Level of Support: Involvement	Low Level of Support: Indifference or Opposition

Characteristics of Relationship:

• This is an ideal working situation. The overlap in relationships between the network and Human Resources is understood, explicit, and incorporated into the activities of both. • Networks with this level of support often cosponsor events with Human Resources and work directly with HR and management in designing programs and initiatives. • Externally, some networks are concerned at this point about being seen as too closely tied to Human Resources. There is a definite need to establish the network's independence.	• Networks with this level of support usually work with Human Resources on certain areas, but small tensions over role overlap arise more frequently and may have an impact on the network's effectiveness. • This level of support still allows for a significant level of interaction and mutual assistance between the network and Human Resources. • Networks often have a few individuals in Human Resources they work with on activities. You may be less likely to get data from HR, especially numbers regarding women's advancement in the company. However, you'll usually get assistance with noncontroversial topics such as speakers series or seminars. • At this level, it's more difficult to place pressure on Human Resources. While the relationship is strong on issues where HR and the network clearly agree, when the network challenges HR, the response can be more negative.	• The network receives little support from Human Resources and is often unable to get data or information regarding current programs and policies. • Networks with low levels of HR support often operate in environments where gender issues are a low priority or are actively ignored. If there are programs or discussions regarding women, the network may not be included. HR may want to manage the issue without involving the network.

Chart 4.3 Continued

High Level of Support: Championing	Medium Level of Support: Acceptance and Interest	Low Level of Support: Indifference or Opposition
What They Want from the Network:		
• HR uses the network as a conduit for information about women in the company, an adviser for approaches and policies, and a "reality check" for certain data or programs. • Women's networks can also pilot programs on a small scale, identifying the opportunities and challenges and making recommendations to Human Resources, which can then implement the program on a wider basis.	• This level of support is often similar to a higher level when it relates to what HR expects from the network. However, if the network raises issues HR doesn't consider a priority, the relationship can become more difficult.	• Human Resources usually wants the network to involve itself only in activities that don't affect HR. The more you drift into HR territory, the more actively HR personnel will discourage you.
What the Network Can Expect from Human Resources:		
• Networks receive more or less automatic financial support, meeting space, and other operational assistance. • Human Resources will more often consider and implement a network's recommendations.	• Networks receive some operational support from Human Resources (financial, space, and so on) when the interests of the two groups are congruent. • More confidential company data may not be available to networks. • You have the opportunity to "sell" an issue to Human Resources but your audience may be more skeptical. It takes more hard data and more support from above to convince HR to work with the network on an issue.	• Networks receive little operational support. • HR is unlikely to provide data for the network or to collaborate on programs or initiatives.

Chart 4.3 Continued

High Level of Support: Championing	Medium Level of Support: Acceptance and Interest	Low Level of Support: Indifference or Opposition

Options and Strategies:

• Use your high level of support wisely. Go to HR only for activities that most require HR involvement. • While you will want to cosponsor some external events with Human Resources, you don't want to appear to be just another arm of HR. Work to create external opportunities to reinforce the separate identity of the network.	• Establish a good track record with HR. Effective networks pick and choose early projects to work with Human Resources on and ensure that those projects work smoothly. The goal is to prove that the group is trustworthy, understanding, and effective. • Occasionally, networks can enlist senior-level support to improve this relationship. Handle this delicately, though. You don't want HR staff to think you're going behind their backs. • Create an open communications line between the network and HR so any potential problems can be identified and addressed early.	• It's helpful to approach HR professionals individually to build support. • If you have a higher level of support from senior managers, then ask them to informally reach out to Human Resources.

Include Human Resources Staff on Network Committees. Some networks decide that meeting with HR every few months isn't enough. Especially if you need HR assistance with the detailed workings of committees, you may want to have some HR staffers as formal members of the committee. This may automatically happen if there are a number of network members who are also in Human Resources. If this isn't the case, consider creating a HR liaison to certain committees requiring resources and assistance.

> Women in engineering initiated a women's forum and developed action committees from it. No HR person was associated with any of those groups and so the question became, "Where are you going with this?" We asked that each committee have an HR adviser. It didn't have to be a person doing stuff on a committee, but someone just to make sure that they had the resources, that they were developing something that would be acceptable to management.
>
> *—Women's network leader*

Working with Human Resources: Patience Is a Virtue

If you're like most women's networks, you want to do things *now*. However, there are times when Human Resources doesn't work that way.

> We helped develop some of the private programs, the prototypes, but it seems like it takes such a long item to institutionalize. We've got such good ideas but then it's got to be okayed by HR. If it was ours, we'd have it developed already and have women in there. It just takes time and I guess you have to have patience.
>
> *—Women's network leader*

Remember that HR may be right about its sense of timing—there are often multiple hoops to jump through in an organization. The best advice is to be patient and recognize that HR usually knows how to move a recommendation through the organization. Remember, HR support is critical.

If you feel that it could move more quickly, offer your assistance but recognize there may be barriers you're not aware of. A final option is to involve senior leaders if you feel that HR is purposely slowing down the process. However, that's sometimes a politically unwise solution and can result in further resistance. Understand that approval takes time and be sure to move forward with other activities in the meantime.

As this statement highlights, HR can also provide a perspective on management opinion. Especially if you're just starting out, you may need the political savvy of HR professionals to help you understand if a recommendation will be accepted or rejected.

MEMO TO HR:

You may feel that women in the organization are pushing for action before the company culture is ready, but keep in mind that these employees are also working for the good of the entire organization. They deserve not only your support and understanding but also—and especially—the insider knowledge you possess.

Building Support Beyond the Big Three

As we mentioned at the beginning of the chapter, there are other groups besides top and middle management and HR that the network needs to connect with:

- Other employee networks at the organization
- Diversity councils or task forces addressing gender issues
- Employees as a whole who are not directly involved in the network
- Men in the company
- Women outside the network (by choice or due to membership limits)

Once the network has established a presence in the organization, you can more easily reach out to the next tier of audiences. To that end, we have included more detailed information and strategies to build support among these groups in Chapter Six.

MEMO TO HR:

Facilitating interaction among networks can foster more employee cooperation and help all networks achieve their common goals. While a diversity council is a formal manifestation of this spirit, informal interaction between established networks can be another way to help people work well together.

The following strategies can help you lay the groundwork for more active outreach to these groups:

Other Employee Networks

Identifying shared goals and ways to work together is the most successful strategy. The challenge is to identify discrete roles so you don't end up doing the same work.

> One of the most effective things we're doing is we're working with the black employee network to combine efforts for a mentoring program. The black network and the women's council believed that mentoring should be available to everybody at all levels of the organization . . . we joined forces. The two groups have gotten together and defined the goals and defined the process. It's been a nice approach to working together on a common issue.
>
> —*Women's network leader*

Since many of the issues are shared, it can be difficult to prevent networks from stumbling over each other in addressing their needs. Additionally, some employee networks feel they are competing with each other for limited company resources and attention. To minimize that, consider building relationships individually across networks. Often, leaders of networks will meet informally to discuss goals and activities. From that can spring cosponsored events or combined recommendations to management.

Diversity Councils

These are becoming more and more common in organizations across the country. Women's networks are natural members of those councils since they represent women in the organization. At their best, these councils are effective tools to combine viewpoints from a range of sources and present united recommendations to management.

> We have a pluralism council and there are members from each of the resource groups on that council, plus one or two members from each of the divisions. The focus isn't so much to get the groups to work together, as it is to promote pluralism and diversity in general.
>
> —*Women's network leader*

However, it can be difficult to achieve this desired end result because of internal conflicts and changing membership.

> With the diversity council, every year it changes. They wipe out all the members that have been there one year and start fresh the next year. So it's really

hard to work with them because you get going on something and then the next year they do everything differently.

—Women's network leader

The success of your participation in a diversity council often hinges on your relationships with Human Resources (the usual manager for such councils) and employee groups (the other participants.) Participation in these groups can sometimes be frustrating due to the amount of consensus required, but when done well, they can be a powerful voice for change within the organization.

Other Employees in the Organization

While this group may not be a direct audience for the network, many would be interested in your programs and will benefit from them. Additionally, the more support you have among the general employee population, the more legitimate and credible the network becomes.

To build employee support, consider programs that highlight the assistance the network provides to them. For example, a speakers series on current business issues can be open to all employees and publicized as such. A seminar on management skills can be held at a time when a wide audience can attend. Some women's networks operating in an economically uncertain environment hold résumé workshops or transitioning events to reinforce the point that the network benefits the whole organization, not just women.

Post newsletters or mailings in public areas to educate the larger employee population about the network and its mission. Communication activities like these provide employees with the correct language to use when describing and evaluating the women's group—a critical issue, because informal discussions about the network are bound to take place throughout the organization on an ongoing basis, and network publicity can make a great deal of difference in the tone of those discussions.

Men in the Company

Many of the same lessons apply here as apply for employees in general. Men are more likely to be skeptical of the group's goals and purpose. As it is crucial to educate men on why a women's network is needed—that is, what it is in the work environment that makes women want and need to form a network—it is also important to convince them that the network will benefit them. Larger events that include men can help the network do that.

We felt that holding a parenting seminar changed our image a lot. We didn't realize the benefit of events like that, but it was very successful and seventy-five of the parents that participated were men.

—Women's network leader

Women Outside the Network

These women come in two categories: they are not members of the network either by *choice* or by *necessity.*

Building support among the first group involves understanding why they aren't members. Often it's because of a lack of time. To address that, consider having programs or events that require little time commitment and have large payoffs. For example, the network can create a pamphlet on designing a flexible work arrangement. Women interested in it can simply read the pamphlet and pick up practical tips instead of sitting through a lecture on the topic. By focusing on low-intensity activities that reinforce the direct benefits of the network, you may be able to persuade these women to join.

Building support among women who aren't members because they don't fulfill membership requirements is more difficult. Nevertheless, ignoring these women can generate a backlash. Often there are ways to reach out to them and even encourage them to form a women's network targeted to their needs. By doing that you are able to retain your focus on a certain level or group of women, while not ignoring the issues facing women in different parts of the organization.

Summary

Every organization includes several separate audiences that can provide critical support for the women's network. The range of approaches differs for each group, but a number of basic strategies underlie them all:

- Reinforce the business case for the network and how it helps the bottom line.
- Clearly outline how the network can directly benefit the particular audience.
- Leverage support from different areas to gain support among skeptical groups.
- Use a variety of informal and formal communication vehicles.
- Think about building support as a long-term effort.

The key step is positioning the network as a contributor to individual and organizational success. If you can do that well, you'll have far fewer problems gaining support throughout the organization.

Checklist

☐ Identify the key groups in the organization needed for support and the main players and decision makers within each group:

    ____ Top management

    ____ Middle management

    ____ Human Resources

    ____ Other employee networks

    ____ Diversity councils

    ____ Employees throughout the organization

    ____ Men in the company

    ____ Women outside the network

☐ Determine the current level of support from each group.

☐ Examine how their level of support will help or hinder the network.

☐ Set priorities regarding where to establish greater support in the short term and the long term.

☐ Design strategies to develop that support.

☐ Decide whether the level of support requires that you modify any of the network's goals or activities.

CHAPTER FIVE

YOU'VE ARRIVED!
PUTTING YOUR PLANS INTO ACTION

Guiding Question: How can the network design and implement effective activities and programs supporting its goals and mission?

All the activities we've described so far—deciding on a mission, building support among management, and communicating to members—have been acts of creation: creating the base of support necessary for the network to realize its goals. That's an exciting process, but it can be frustrating, too—none of it directly addresses the factors that led people to start thinking of a network in the first place. Once that groundwork has been done, however, you can move on to the most visible and satisfying form of action—the programs, activities, and events that people picture when they think about an established women's network. This chapter is designed to help you construct events and programs that fulfill the network's mission and goals.

Regardless of their network's stage of development, network leaders and members will find something useful in this chapter. For newer networks, there are events designed to introduce the network. More experienced networks will find it helpful for its evaluation tools. Older networks may be ready for larger-scale events such as conferences, which we cover in detail. By the end of this chapter, you will have all the tools and information you need to put on successful activities.

We've organized the chapter into the four most common major categories of activity, plus one area that is more of a role than an activity per se:

- Networking
- Career development

- High-visibility activities
- Community outreach
- Advising management and Human Resources

This last activity falls into a special category. It doesn't involve events, public or otherwise, but it can widen the impact of a network to affect the company as a whole.

Overlap, obviously, is common. For example, if you're organizing a program that pairs senior women in the company with more junior women for mentoring and support, you're fulfilling two categories—networking and career development. Other activities such as conferences can cover even more categories.

Event Success Factors

Despite the different skills and strategies involved in different events, there are a few overarching success factors that run through them all. We will use these as guideposts throughout the chapter.

1. *Meet specific needs of network members.* This may seem obvious—but you'd be surprised how often it's ignored. Linking the activities and events of the network to the needs and interests of its members is not only critical to the success of events, it is also necessary to ensure the long-term health of the network. If members aren't going to be interested in an event, don't spend valuable time and energy putting it on.

> As far as the programs are concerned, the content is what sells. If people are really interested in the topic, they'll be there.
>
> —*Women's network leader*

2. *Effectively communicate the event and its purpose.* No matter how outstanding an event is, if no one knows about it, you won't have an audience. Use a wide range of communications tools—and as you design your communications piece, be careful to make it send the right message. Bonus: *In addition to its effectiveness at building an audience, event publicity is one of the best ways to educate the company about the network.* Flyers posted on company bulletin boards, e-mail sent to managers, and notices in the company newsletter all serve to increase awareness of the network, even among those who are not involved in its activities.

3. *Design a clear objective—and then measure an event's effectiveness.* Smart networks design activities and programs with clear objectives in mind. If you're organizing

a cocktail reception for network members and female board members, be explicit about why you want everyone to get together. Is it to familiarize the board members with the network's mission and objectives? Is it to create opportunities for network members to establish ties to the board? Whatever the goal, be sure to state it clearly. Then measure whether you have met it. You have a range of options for measuring the effectiveness of your activities. Some, like surveys or informal discussions, will be familiar from the discussion of the climate survey. Others may be new to you. Throughout this chapter, we will be summarizing the evaluation tools you can use for various events.

4. *Involve senior leaders in the company.* Senior management doesn't need to attend every event, but you do want to let them know what you're doing. Your method can be as simple as sending them a copy of the invitation. You can also regularly communicate updates on recent events and activities. Your events are an important way to communicate the network's mission and goals—keeping senior leaders aware of what you want as well as of what you're doing.

Tips for Event Managers

As you begin planning your activities, bear in mind that the event itself is a communication tool. Especially if you have a newer network, any event or program you put on will get some attention; it will also communicate the tone and purpose of the network. Successful networks choose events accordingly. Some groups decide to organize events for broader audiences early on, to send the message that they benefit the company as a whole. Other networks focus on women-only events to reinforce the need for women to build networks. Whatever the message is, be sure your events send it.

Don't forget about events that strengthen the network. Clearly, network activities are designed to help the members. However, it's easy to get caught up in external programs, like a speakers series or "Take Our Daughters to Work" day, and allow internal network activities to take on a lower priority, eventually weakening the network infrastructure and its events and programs. Be sure to keep the network's strength in mind as you plan events, and don't forget such basics as membership drives and regular meetings.

Be realistic! By now, this refrain has started to sound familiar, but it bears repeating. While the temptation may be to accomplish everything right away, the time and resources usually can't be marshaled in one year. It's OK to sequence your activities over a few years—and you'll be less likely to experience the dreaded member burnout.

> **Beware of Burnout**
>
> Be selfish with your time. That's one of the golden rules when it comes to or-
> ganizing events. The key is to identify your goals and needs, choosing the ac-
> tivities to meet the most goals at once. With member burnout a major
> challenge for networks—everyone is busy, after all—it's critical to focus your
> activities first on what members need, and second on what the company
> needs. Remember, the members will be doing all the work. If they don't see a
> payoff for their efforts, they'll be less likely to volunteer another time.

Networking Events

When Catalyst surveyed women's networks about their roles and activities, the most frequent responses centered on classic networking events. Usually the most important goal of these events is the *sharing of information*. Networks organize events where participants can pool information about business opportunities, career strategies, or new company developments. They also set up opportunities for participants to share more personal information, like strategies for balancing work and personal responsibilities or frustrations about barriers in the organization.

The key to successful networking events is to keep them focused. You'll want some opportunities for free-form discussions and open conversation. Too many unfocused activities, however, can lead to frustration because the specific needs of members are not met. So in addition to having those open networking opportunities, be sure to organize more targeted events.

There are two ways to think about targeting events. The first is identifying your goals. The second is identifying the groups in the organization with whom you want to network. Creating these two lists is a helpful exercise which will result in a more focused set of options—which is useful, given the wide variety of types of events that vie for a network's attention.

Common Goals for Networking Events

- Development of a regular group of members and interested parties to discuss issues women face in the company
- Establishment of informal relationships between network members and various groups within the company
- Increased visibility of network members with managers and senior managers
- Formation or reinforcement of relationships among network members

- Building links with other employee groups or networks outside the company
- Increased knowledge of strategies for advancement
- Education of company about network and mission

Common Groups Included in Networking Events

- Network members
- Women at the company who are not members
- Managers
- Senior executives
- Board members, female and male
- Company employees
- Other employee networks, inside or outside the company
- Current or potential clients
- Women in the community or professional groups in the area

Another important factor to think about is the *intensity* of the event. When it comes to networking events, there is a wide range of possibilities. An informal brown-bag lunch once a month is relatively easy to set up. Organizing a formal reception with senior managers each quarter requires significantly more planning.

And remember—you don't have to set up events for members to network. Tools such as member directories, once created, can be used by members to network on their own.

We have a network book with names and pictures, that is distributed to all members. It's permission to call anyone in the book and then ask them, "Would you have lunch with me?" or "Would you have a cup of coffee with me?"

—*Women's network leader*

Some technologically advanced women's networks have even set up electronic chat rooms or discussion lists for members and interested parties to discuss pertinent issues.

We have an electronic address for men or women to sign up for. The impetus is communication about women's issues having to do with business at the company. The group starts discussion about activities, networking opportunities, or other information. Then individuals sign up for those issues that come across. The core groups keep the information fed.

—*Women's network leader*

What to Do?

Here's a quick reference list of some of the most common networking activities. (For more detail, see Chart 2.1 at the end of Chapter Two.)

- Create a membership directory with background information about members' positions, interests, and experiences.
- Set up on-line chat rooms or bulletin boards for discussions.
- Hold receptions with members and other groups in the organization such as women on the board, senior executives, members of other networks, or managers.
- Organize a speakers series with opportunities for discussions before or after speech.
- Hold evening or weekend social events, such as dinners or retreats.
- Hold a cocktail reception with network members and female clients or colleagues.
- Meet with other women's networks in the area or with community groups that share your mission.

Don't forget that network meetings themselves can be opportunities to network. Reserve some time during meetings for members to get to know each other, especially if you have a newer network.

Success Factors: Meeting Your Members' Needs

Some members want career advice, others are interested in learning about work/life strategies, still others want a group of women to call upon for advice. Because there is such a range of interests, it's important to create a wide range of activities.

That doesn't mean you have to create four sets of concurrent networking events. Instead, consider having a regular networking lunch with varying topics. One month you can discuss how to find a career coach. Another month focus on flexible schedules. There are a number of benefits to such a standing event. First, not every member feels an obligation to attend each lunch. Second, there's a great deal of flexibility in topics and discussions. Finally, it's a way to further stabilize the network. Knowing there is a regular date for the network luncheon eliminates scheduling problems and reinforces the network's long-term nature.

We have brown-bag lunches to talk about things we like to talk about. For example, another member and I do one for women with small children where we can just get together and wallow in all of our little details. And then we have a general lunch the third Thursday of every month where anyone could come and talk. We do it right in the middle of the executive dining room.

—Women's network leader

Success Factors: Effective Publicity

If you're organizing a brown-bag lunch to discuss the company's recent merger, make that explicit. You'll avoid having participants show up who expect to discuss flexible work options. Be sure to be specific as to the topic of discussion, the leaders (if any) who will be present, the purpose of the event (networking, career development, or whatever), and any other relevant details.

We invite everyone through posters and notices in the company newsletter, and when you log into the computers there's a notice about that networking event.

—Women's network leader

Success Factors: Defining and Measuring Effectiveness

It's sometimes difficult to evaluate informal networking events. How do you know whether members are networking effectively with one another? Most often, it's the informal feedback you receive after the events that can help you judge. Your job is to make sure that information gets to you, perhaps by actively reaching out to participants and soliciting their opinions. Because one-to-one feedback is time-consuming, it is best confined to the aftermath of smaller events.

For larger events, networks often put together *follow-up surveys.* These ask about goals for the events, effectiveness of programming, and future interests of members. You may not want to do this for every event because of the energy required, but surveys are helpful tools for evaluating the event and planning future ones. Surveys like this are often distributed at the events themselves, with the request that they be filled out before participants leave. That way the feedback is fresh and more surveys get handed in.

We hand out a four- or five-question survey at our events and we ask them to rate what they've just participated in. How did you like it? What did you like? What didn't you like? How useful was it? What would you like to see in terms of events or topics for the next event? So we get instantaneous feedback.

—Women's network leader

Finally, a simple head count can be a good measuring tool. If members attend events in large numbers, you know you're on the right track. A drop in audience size might indicate the reverse.

Success Factors: Involving the Company's Senior Leaders

If you're organizing an event to introduce senior leaders to network members, then, obviously, those leaders will be directly involved. Your goal might be to increase the visibility of women in the network, hence your primary objective would be to include important managers and executives.

> There are a lot of good people in this organization and I need to find them. Through the network's mentoring program and networking events, I have access to people when I'm thinking about advancement and succession planning.
>
> *—Management liaison*

On the other hand, if it's a networking event for members, then senior leaders should simply know that the event exists. You probably don't even want them

---

Women on Board: McGraw-Hill

More than eighty women met McGraw-Hill's two female directors at a luncheon given by the firm's Women in Management Network in December of 1997. The network members had an opportunity to engage in discussion and exchange views with the two board members, as well as to hear about their career paths and to get their advice on various issues that concern women in the corporation.

Women in Management sent out e-mail notes to 350 people to announce the event, then followed up with paper invitations. (They also reported on it afterward on the company's intranet.) While they were concerned about how "free and open" the discussion would be if they invited men, they decided that anyone could come (although they specifically invited only those on their mailing list).

The discussion covered a range of topics, including strategies for women to use in advancing their careers. And afterward, a large number of women approached the board members for private conversation—a measure of how open these women were and how helpful their advice had been.

to attend, so confine your liaison to copying them on the event publicity or giving them an overview of the purpose and results of the event.

Career Development Events

Many women join networks because they are interested in learning about how to advance their own careers, gain a mentor, or participate in other career development activities. Others join because they want to have a say in how career development systems for the company are designed. It is these two goals that drive much of the career development effort for networks.

Most networks focus first on programs for the individual—with the emphasis on giving women necessary information and tools for advancing within the organization. Activities can range from the more general, like seminars or speakers series, to the more personal, such as one-to-one mentoring programs or coaching opportunities. Newer networks often overlap career development events and networking events, such as setting up a luncheon where women can network and share career strategies. This is a perfect example of creating one event to fulfill two network goals.

> If you want to get ahead or if you want to get a different kind of job or be in a different part of the business, you need to accept responsibility for your own career development. We try to do things in support of that. We've brought people in to talk about positioning yourself in the future and taking responsibility for your own development.
>
> *—Women's network leader*

The second area of career development is somewhat more complex. As networks identify the issues that concern women in their organizations, they often uncover systemic barriers related to how employees are recruited, developed, and advanced. To address those challenges, women's networks often work directly with executives and with Human Resources to help them understand where improvement is needed. As you can imagine, this area overlaps with the activities of "Advising management and Human Resources." In fact, the effectiveness of these activities is driven primarily by a network's success in advising management. We'll return to this issue in the next section of this chapter.

There are often opportunities to lead task forces or report on analyzed data, and these experiences can help broaden members' abilities. While this may not be an overt goal of the network, it should be highlighted and recognized when it occurs. Being a member of a network can act as an alternate skills development opportunity, especially for entry-level and mid-level members, and can be a way to encourage their involvement.

> Being part of the network provides business experience and growth experience for women that you don't get in the workplace when you're not in any management position—how to work with people, how to deal with conflict, how to resolve issues. . . .
>
> —*Women's network leader*

The concept of *partnership* comes up frequently when thinking about the career development activities of women's networks. The networks improve the organization while helping women to develop. But the partnership means that the network will need support and resources from the organization to strengthen the skills of its members.

Career development events can't ensure a promotion for a member. However, these seminars and programs can be a critical part of developing members' skills and ensuring their preparedness for increased responsibilities and opportunities. Designing effective programs that are clearly communicated, evaluated, and publicized to management can reenergize members and reinforce the network's impact on women in the organization.

What to Do?

Here's a quick reference list of some of the most common career development activities:

- Speakers series focusing on career management and skills development
- Workshops or seminars (time management, public speaking, and so on)
- Leadership opportunities within the network
- Mentoring programs within the network
- Informal coaching opportunities
- Resource libraries on career-related topics
- Formal opportunities to discuss career development
- Leadership forums highlighting success strategies for executives or senior women
- Directory of career development resources within the company and outside

Types of Career Development Programs

It's helpful to group different types of career development programs based on your goals. Most activities tend to fall into the following areas:

• *Events providing information about how to advance in the organization.* These include informal networking conversations, "how to manage your career" speakers, and formal presentations by Human Resources staff to discuss career paths and success stories. Networks also bring in a number of external speakers on career development topics. Such events or seminars are often relatively easy to set up, provided you have the funds for the speaker, and can be very beneficial to members. The most formal and involved of these events are often cosponsored with HR and highlight successful women and their strategies as well as informing members about the formal HR systems in the organization.

• *Events providing specific, often technical, information about the business itself.* Networks recognize that employees need to be aware of the latest advances in their field. To ensure their members are up to speed, many networks are increasing the number of career development events focusing on specific skills or knowledge related to their industry. Most commonly, this involves bringing in an outside speaker who can review the latest information and convey future directions in this area.

These events shouldn't be limited to speakers from outside the company. Someone from the outside may know a great deal about the topic, but can only know so much about the organization. Your own vice president of operations may not only tell you the technical information but translate that into how it affects the organization and you directly. Bonus: *Such an event can be more evidence to senior leadership that the network is business-focused.* It also, of course, creates opportunities for members to network with upper management.

• *One-to-one programs providing direct feedback to individuals about their careers.* These programs are often the most requested; they are also the most difficult to implement. Putting together a mentoring program requires a pretty significant commitment of time and resources. Before jumping into a program like this, consider whether it needs to be formal or not. Many groups create networking events with the explicit goal of encouraging mentoring relationships. The more senior women attending the event agree in advance to act as coaches, and the more junior women know it's up to them to seek out a potential mentor.

Another factor to consider is how to involve Human Resources and managers. After all, once you start providing feedback to network members on career goals, you start to intrude on the manager's job of review and promotion and on HR's role in career development. Successful networks link their mentoring programs to HR and keep managers in the loop.

Caveat: Because such programs are so complicated, networks probably shouldn't tackle formal mentoring programs or formal career development interventions until they've been in existence for one to two years and are truly well-established.

MEMO TO HR:

You don't have to do everything yourselves. In this area as in others, women's networks can make your job less burdensome, and help the employees you are responsible for become more skilled.

Success Factors: Meeting Your Members' Needs

Some women may be interested in learning new technical skills. Others may be interested in hearing about new company development programs. Still others may want more direct feedback about their own careers. It can be difficult to meet these different goals through one or two programs. Because of that, it's important to prioritize. You should have a relatively detailed sense of what members are interested in from your climate survey, so try to pick up what's most important first.

Success Factors: Effective Publicity

Publicizing career development events is often a very straightforward process involving getting the word out on the topic, date, and time. Most employees enjoy taking advantage of whatever career development opportunities there are; they'll come to an event ready to get anything they can out of it.

The only exception is with the more formal career coaching opportunities. In the case of mentoring programs, it's critical to be explicit about expectations for both mentors and their protégés. People need to recognize that a mentor can advise them, but can't create opportunities for them. Mentors need to recognize that they can't shape an individual's career, only pass along knowledge and advice. Strong mentoring programs spend a great deal of time discussing expected results and how to achieve them.

Success Factors: Defining and Measuring Effectiveness

Again, with the larger career development events, the most effective evaluation tools are often surveys. It's too time-consuming to ask people individually about the event, and a survey can cover a number of topics. Be sure to ask about the relevance of the topic, the effectiveness of the speaker or seminar leader, how the session will help individuals with their jobs, ways to improve the event in the future, and their other event ideas. These results will help you prove the impact of the event as well as give you ideas for future programs.

You also want to be sure you get enough surveys back. Event organizers often include surveys in materials given out at the registration table or leave surveys on chairs, being sure to ask for them back before participants leave the program. *Questions that address very specific issues can be extremely useful.* One women's network asked, "How will this event help you next week in your job?" The positive feedback this question generated made it easier to prove the specific benefits the network provided to members.

> At our career group events we have surveys on the chairs and we ask people to fill them out and drop them in a box on their way out. We ask why did you come, what were your expectations about the speakers, what did you think the quality of the program was, what would you like to see more of, and would you be willing to plan an event. We asked also, because both of our events have been on-site and paid by the company, would you like to go to an outside event and would you be willing to pay. Then we leave a good block for comments, which is the really fun stuff. We've had people write letters. That's been really helpful to our committee. We've also got names and phone numbers of women who want to get more involved.
>
> —*Women's network leader*

But don't end your evaluation there. Many times career development events have important *implicit* goals. You may have a speaker series on globalization with an explicit goal of educating members and employees. However, your implicit goal may be to reinforce the network's focus on current business issues. To achieve that goal, you want the event to reach a wide audience, you want executives to know about the event, and you want executives to know of the impact of the event. The event itself is a communications vehicle, so be sure to evaluate that aspect of it, too.

Success Factors: Involving the Company's Senior Leaders

Having a senior executive introduce the network's week-long series on managing your career or having a senior executive as the keynote speaker for workshops on emerging trends in your industry can add a certain luster and will certainly beef up the attendance. But many networks haven't reached that point of acceptance, and certainly many executives have little time to devote to these activities. Try to target certain high-visibility events and ensure an executive attends. And of course, it's essential to have executives as participants in some career development programs.

One of the things we focused on was shadowing and mentoring for the women at the company because we didn't have any female mentors. That's been pretty successful in terms of participation by top management. The CEO in particular has made opportunities for women to shadow him for an entire week.

—Women's network leader

One women's network created a mentoring program for their senior women members, lining up mentors for them among still more senior company executives. There were numerous benefits from this program. The executives could provide critical career advice and were also more likely to be in a position where they could "make things happen" for the women in the program. Bonus: *In the course of participating in the mentoring program the executives saw the positive impact of the network and became that much more vocal champions of the group itself.* Also, as visible mentors these executives sent the message throughout the organization that coaching and mentoring were important jobs of managers and executives.

As always, whether you gain their attendance or involvement or not, communicating with senior leaders about your activities is crucial. If a one-to-one meeting isn't possible, you can at least summarize the activities and the impact in a written version and circulate it to involved executives.

Don't Reinvent the Wheel: How to Take Advantage of Career Development Programs Inside and Outside Your Organization

Once you've identified the needs of the network members, try tapping into already-existing programs, rather than creating them from scratch. Does your company have a Training and Development department? Are there career development seminars? If there is no list of such events for employees, then approach that office directly or create that list yourself. Ask people in Training and Development how they might be able to help. If they don't have the programs you need, they may at least be a good resource for outside speakers or resources.

Also think about community organizations. Many women's networks cosponsor events with the local Toastmasters or YWCA. Your members can also participate in other women's networks outside the company—community-based or trade or business-based. When you find appropriate outside career development events, publicize them. Your members will be happy to learn about these opportunities, and the local groups will gain increased participation in their events.

High-Visibility Activities

Annual conferences, companywide dinners, "Take Our Daughters to Work" days, Women's History Month celebrations—they all make a splash. Such events are a great way to energize members, reach a wide audience, and increase the visibility of the network and its members. They can also highlight issues important to the network and show off management support of the network.

Obviously, events like these also require a great deal of work and resources. Because they are so visible, it's important to have them run smoothly. Lining up speakers, arranging for conference facilities, organizing participants, involving management, negotiating for funding, and all the other hundreds of details can be overwhelming if you don't have enough staff.

> There is an expectation that you will kill yourself to do these full-blown events. I think by both men and women in the company, there's an expectation that it will be done really well.
>
> —*Women's network leader*

If you plan carefully, though, and give yourself enough lead time, you can ensure a successful event.

> We had a food fair where we had each of our business groups represented. We had new products and they gave out samples. We had hundreds of people come to that and it got so big that it was scary. But it was really nice because it got a lot of participation out of men and women and it brought a lot of people together.
>
> —*Women's network leader*

> Every year we have an annual conference on company time. All the women above a certain level are invited to attend a day-long series of seminars. Our chairman and also the president of our sector were there. They spent time with us in the afternoon answering questions. We had almost four hundred women attend that.
>
> —*Women's network leader*

The key is in the planning. Spend time early on scoping out the event and what you want to accomplish. Once you've identified your desired end result, work backward and ask yourself the following questions:

What to Do?

Here's a quick reference list of some productive high-visibility activities:

- Annual network conference with seminars, speakers (internal and external), and networking sessions
- Celebrations of Women's History Month—speakers throughout the month, events for members, companywide events, educational materials (posters, displays, and so on)
- "Take Our Daughters to Work" day
- Large events for all employees at the company—career development fairs, new product seminars

- How much time do we need to spend planning and executing this event?
- How many people do we need to organize and run the event? (Don't forget about the people you'll need during the event itself to handle registration, AV equipment, participant questions, and all the other issues that come up throughout the event.)
- What level of funding will we require and from whom will we get it?
- What other groups or company resources can we call on for help?
- What should be the tone of the event?
- Who should be invited—all employees, all women, managers, executives?
- How will we sell the event?
- Is this a one-time event or an annual or biannual occurrence?

Giving yourself enough time, staffing, and funding will minimize wear and tear on organizers. Remember, the goal is to enjoy the event yourself, and burning out a month in advance doesn't help. Some networks hire outside consultants to organize events like this, recognizing that they don't have time themselves to devote to it. If you have the resources available to do that, it can make the process easier.

Success Factors: Meeting Your Members' Needs

Usually events like these are made up of many smaller seminars and networking events. As you plan the overall series of activities, return to the goals you have in these areas and ensure your event planning mirrors them. Especially with larger events that run for several days, it's good to balance high- and low-intensity activities. You'll want to have speakers on important company topics, but you also want some low-key, humorous speakers or low-energy events. That way, participants aren't exhausted by the end. You'll also want to combine listening activities, such as keynote speakers, with participatory activities, such as small group discussions. Have social events, but don't go overboard with them—constant networking can be draining and doesn't necessarily create the right feel for the event.

Success Factors: Effective Publicity

As you can imagine, good publicity is key to the success of these events. You want a large turnout, and that requires a range of publicity strategies. You want to tailor your message and vehicle to the various groups to ensure the message gets through and inspires them to participate. Here are some strategies aimed at the various audiences:

Managers. Since this group is often the busiest in the organization, to gain their participation you need to prove how the event will directly benefit them. Construct publicity materials that highlight the skills they can gain or ideas they can take back to their jobs. Another effective strategy is to highlight the executives who will be in attendance. If the boss (or better yet, the boss's boss) is attending, it will most likely be in the target manager's best interest to attend as well.

Employees in General. As with managers, if you can prove the direct benefits of the event, you're halfway there.

> We put on a health fair, a women's health fair, to which the entire corporation was invited. In inviting the whole corporation, we said to the men, "We all know you have women in your lives. You really need to be concerned about women's health issues." And it was a very successful program.
>
> —*Women's network leader*

To reach this very large group, you need to employ a range of strategies. Use company bulletin boards, distribute your newsletter, include event listings in the company newsletter, announce the event through e-mail, and post announcements throughout the organization. Think about how major companywide events are publicized and use those same vehicles.

Some events require that individuals from different offices and regions attend. Especially at annual conferences for the network, you will most likely be drawing from members in various locations. This raises an additional set of planning questions and requires a broader communications strategy. Publicizing the event in various locations requires increased coordination as well as increased funding.

However, a successful event that gathers members from various locations has a larger impact on membership.

Success Factors: Defining and Measuring Effectiveness

The larger goals of network events are often to reinforce cohesion among members, increase visibility for the network, gain increased support for the group and its mission, and educate the company and participants about key issues. Smaller goals are related to the individual events themselves. Networking events have different goals from those of their keynote speeches. During your planning, identify the range of goals you have and think about internal consistency. If your list of goals is massive and doesn't have a clear theme or two running through it, that's a sign that you may be trying to do too much in one event. Try streamlining some of the events so that a few consistent messages come through.

An exhibit for Women's History Month can be difficult to evaluate. However, there are ways to do it. For an exhibit, consider having a notebook at the end for participants to write their thoughts in. If you're organizing a "Take Our Daughters to Work" day, have each parent and daughter write a paragraph about their experiences. For a larger conference or series of events, consider short surveys or individual follow-up. One women's conference focused their last session on "What Will This Mean on Monday Morning?" as a way to evaluate what participants could take away from the event. Be creative in the ways you measure impact.

Success Factors: Involving the Company's Senior Leaders

As we mentioned earlier, it's important to be strategic in how you involve executives. Ideally, you'd like to involve certain leaders as keynote speakers or to kick off the series of events. They should be alerted as early as possible, so the event gets on their calendar. Think early about who those individuals should be and target your efforts accordingly.

> We have five key executives whose calendars we've been asked to work around. So when we plan an event, we make sure those people are in town and it gets on their calendars early.
>
> *—Women's network leader*

Senior leaders usually can't attend an entire conference. However, they can attend certain seminars and can be visible supporters at those. Think about where you need to show that support and to whom. Senior leaders can also provide critical and useful advice during the planning stages. Once you've outlined where you need their involvement, approach a range of executives and ask them for their participation.

Dow's WOWs

The Women's Opportunity Workshops put on by the Dow Chemical Women's Innovation Network fulfill all the criteria for successful high-visibility activities, and according to the network head, they "really put the network on the map." The first event the network attempted in reaching out to Dow women was a quarterly speakers series featuring senior women as well as a female board member, to which all employees were invited. The only problem with that kind of invitation is that if the event appeals to more people than the room will hold, you end up with disgruntled would-be attendees. Despite attempts to videotape the speeches for later viewing, the Dow network kept hearing from disappointed women who wanted to get in for the live event and couldn't.

Realizing that there was no way they could include all employees in any such activity, the network decided to create a major conference, in the form of a workshop offering management exposure, career skills, and an opportunity for networking. Such an in-depth experience could only be brought off if attendance was by invitation only.

Planning

The network leader put a team together to make the event happen. The team knew they'd never get funding or participation without management support, so the first item on their agenda was selling the leaders of Dow's business groups on the event. After the network team aligned the goals and purposes of the workshop with Dow's core values, which include focusing on employee development, the leaders couldn't really say no—in fact, they played a strong role in choosing participants and they participated themselves.

Next the team, feeling that the only way to carry out a focused and meaningful event was to have a somewhat homogeneous audience, decided to limit attendance to exempt women only. (Yes, there was some backlash, but the next workshop was conceived and executed by and for office professionals such as secretaries and the like. It was a huge success.) When it came to paring down the invitation list to 250 women, they went to the business group leaders for help, giving each a quota of women based on the size of the group and the number of women in it. The network had certain criteria, too: the women needed to have been at Dow for at least five years and they needed to have the potential for long-term Dow careers.

Execution

The goals for the network were to make the event "inspirational and motivational." To that end, the conference began with a dinner at which each table had an assigned topic of discussion and at least one senior leader of the company. With the help of a facilitator, participants networked and discussed such substantive issues as building diversity, making mentoring work, and creating a flexible workplace. Advice from the leaders and clear recommendations were the result.

Also on the program was a speech about breaking the glass ceiling. As a result of his research for the speech, the executive who gave it learned a great deal, he said, getting insight into Dow's environment for women and some of his own behavior that wasn't supportive of women's advancement. His speech was inspiring—sending the message that the leadership really cared about these issues. During the dinner the senior leaders who were present were introduced, reinforcing their involvement.

The workshops were held the next day. After a welcome from Dow's CEO, the organizers showed a video they had produced. In it, young girls talked about what it was to be a girl and women at Dow talked about what it was to be a woman at Dow. The girls saw no barriers ahead; the women described the barriers they had faced and how they overcame them.

Dow's head of diversity spoke about diversity strategies, and an outside person addressed the issue of mentoring. And then the breakout sessions—held both in the morning and the afternoon so everyone attended two—began. Topics ranged from "Taking Charge: How to Restore and Maintain Balance" to "Can We Talk? The Impact of Communication Style on Your Professional Image."

Conclusion

The event caused a rethinking of the network's focus. When senior women at the workshop spoke about the sacrifices they'd made, some of the women in the audience were put off—they didn't want to arrange their lives that way. So instead of concentrating on advancing to executive levels, the network decided to focus on helping individuals define their personal goals and work toward them. That approach has a welcome by-product for the network: it removes much of the distinction between different levels in the organization. Generally speaking, the feedback the network received was spectacular— from women, from leaders, and from the organization. Despite the amount of work it required, it was so successful that the women at Dow plan to repeat it every two years from now on.

The Network Reaches out to the Wider Community

Many women's networks take on activities that extend beyond the borders of their organization. Groups become involved with local community organizations and local women's associations. These types of activities can build business, mentoring, and personal relationships across organizations.

Other community activities, though, are designed to help women in the community. These can be women returning to the workforce, younger girls in high school, or women in shelters. Women's networks also organize events such as fundraisers or clothing drives to benefit local organizations.

> We sponsor a lot of mentoring and development programs with the women's center in our community. We also have done a tremendous amount of work in terms of fundraising. We sponsor a run that benefits a clothing closet to help women who are interviewing for jobs.
>
> *—Women's network leader*

There are a number of payoffs from these activities for both the network and its members.

Working together on a charitable community activity can bring women in the network together, helping create strong relationships. As with other network activities, organizing the events provides opportunities for skill development. Bonus: *These activities can build high visibility for the network within the company while they help the company improve its public image.*

Success Factors: Meeting Your Members' Needs

You clearly want to focus your efforts on programs that capitalize on member interest and reinforce the network's mission. Especially in more traditional environments such as engineering or technology, many women's networks partner with HR to increase the pool of women graduating from colleges with relevant degrees by reaching out to the academic community. This indirectly helps the organization increase the numbers of women in its ranks.

As with all public service activities, working in the community can provide a strong sense of fulfillment. Some networks have a subteam focused on community events. That team is usually made up of members who have links to the community and experience or interest in public service. They may set up day events, such as helping clean up a beach or repaint the local women's center.

What to Do?

Here's a quick reference list of some of the most effective community outreach activities:

- Fundraising events to raise money for local shelters or community groups such as the YWCA
- Outreach programs to girls in local high schools or colleges—mentoring programs, internships, and so on
- Targeted recruiting efforts to develop interest among high school girls in careers in science or technology
- Internships for female students at the organization
- Clothing drives for women looking for jobs

These events are often open just to members, but can also be open to employees in general.

Success Factors: Effective Publicity

Publicizing these programs not only increases participation but also reinforces the network's reach beyond the company itself. You can work at placing stories about the events in community newspapers. Be vigilant about getting your women's network the proper credit.

Success Factors: Defining and Measuring Effectiveness

Evaluation can be difficult because the impact is usually a personal one. As with networking sessions, however, a simple head count of participation levels in successive events provides a good index to the effectiveness of the program. In addition, the individual stories and accomplishments (a house built, a woman with a new job) are often excellent testimonials.

Success Factors: Involving the Company's Senior Leaders

If you can convince executives of how these outreach activities can benefit the company's image, you may be able to get their participation, or at least their support. Be sure, in any case, that you inform them of what you're doing in the community.

Advising Management and Human Resources

This kind of activity widens your span of impact from women in the network to all women at the company (and in some cases, employees in general). For many networks, this is some of the most important and interesting work they do.

> We've been instrumental in changing the corporate culture. Five years ago, when I started, very few women had chosen any sort of flexible work arrangements. In our last survey, we found more than four hundred employees involved—and not all of them are women. We're proud that we're getting the message through—slowly but surely.
>
> *—Women's network leader*

> We are an engineering firm and previously the company only looked at a person as a chemical engineer, not as a man or a woman. Now management wants to understand what those differences mean. They look to the women's group to make them understand women engineers' capabilities and the issues they confront.
>
> *—Management liaison*

> A few years ago, the women's group prepared a proposal for parents who need child care assistance. The result is a child care referral service which helps all our employees to be more effective. In fulfilling their role of helping women, they have helped foster advancement for all employees, across gender lines.
>
> *—Management liaison*

It is in this area that the climate survey described in Chapter One proves its worth. Without the knowledge it provides, it is virtually impossible to recommend strategies to executives and HR. The strategies recommended in Chapter Four for building support among management and HR also come in handy here. Without support from those groups, the network's recommendations will have little impact.

Clearly, it's important to cement your relationships with HR and management. It's also important to be realistic about what you can achieve. Of course you want to redesign the recruitment process or revise the performance review system or create a child care center. The question is, can all that really get done in the first year?

There's a paradox here. In the first year of a network's existence, you often have the greatest freedom—but you also have to be the most careful. There is often a groundswell of support for the network among management and a desire to get things done quickly. You need to exercise the utmost care, however, in choosing your objectives that first year. Much of management's opinions about the network will be formed then. Move too quickly and assume too much, and you'll end up squandering your credibility. Move too slowly and request too little, and you end up missing opportunities and may lose credibility. This is a difficult process, but if handled well, you can build support for the network and create strong programs at the same time.

How to Select Activities

The best activities are the ones that will fulfill the following criteria:

1. *Meets the greatest need among women in the organization.* Consider the most important issues facing women in the company. Determine which will make the biggest difference for women and for the company. For example, if the organization is experiencing large rates of turnover among women, then consider focusing on that. Your recommendations will benefit women but will also directly benefit the company and therefore will be heard more readily by management.

2. *Results in specific actions and builds credibility for the network.* As we said earlier, it's important to choose activities that have a realistic chance of being completed. Redesigning the succession planning process in your first year may be unwise. Programs that require a high level of technical or HR knowledge may need to be put on the back burner. Also consider shying away from "sacred cows" or highly controversial programs for the first few years.

Don't forget that the issues you choose to address will directly reflect on the network. Consider the mission of the network as well as the current direction of the company. If your mission is to focus on executive-level women because company leaders are most interested in this group, don't work on a recruitment policy for entry-level women. If everyone at the company is talking about globalization, consider examining women's ability to gain international experience. As with all your activities, align your advice program with your goals and the company's focus.

3. *Capitalizes on management's interest and involvement.* One of the major activities involved in this area is educating management. You'll often have to sell executives on the importance of your issues and the benefits of addressing them. In the meantime, though, take a good look around the executive ranks and identify what areas they're addressing now. Some executives may be members of HR task forces. Others may have gone on record as being champions of mentoring. If you're lucky, the CEO has already communicated his commitment to creating a positive environment for women.

As much as possible, identify areas of overlap between your goals and existing executive activities and capitalize on that. The interviews with executives conducted as part of the climate survey can provide a wealth of useful insights here. The more you can build upon executive interest and involvement, the easier it will be to get your programs off the ground. You can find natural champions for your work and may track down additional resources. You'll have a clearer sense of what executives are looking for and can tailor your short- and long-term goals accordingly.

4. *Reinforces HR's role and leverages its expertise.* As noted in the last chapter, the lines can be blurred between the network's goals and HR's role. You may be advising management on issues in HR's purview. You must walk a fine line between maintaining the detachment to evaluate (and implicitly criticize) the career development systems or practices that have been implemented, and developing the sort of relationship that will engage HR's support for the implementation of long-term strategies. Sometimes these relationships are easy to manage. Other times they can be much more difficult. The benefits of personal relationships between network members and HR staff become very apparent at this point.

> What we tried for the first time, and I think it was very, very helpful to the membership, was educating members on how to create win/win partnerships with the HR organization.
>
> —*Women's network leader*

To create the most positive relationship possible, it's important to recognize where your role ends and HR's begins. HR staff are responsible for all personnel-related systems and practices and that's not negotiable. They also have a great deal of expertise and knowledge about how to implement programs in the organization. Respecting those responsibilities and abilities goes a long way in ensuring a strong connection between the network and HR. The women's group has neither the time nor resources to implement personnel approaches, so relying on HR is critical.

Types of Advisory Activities

There are two major categories of activities in advising management and Human Resources. The first is educating management on issues facing women in the organization.

> Our president seems to see us as a pipeline from him down to the rank and file. From our point of view, we are a pipeline in the other direction. We bring the

issues from the employees in the trenches up to management and make executives aware of them.

—*Women's network leader*

This involves not only letting management know about how women are faring in the company, but also reinforcing management's role. Effective networks don't stop at a description of the problem; they create a specific list of actions for senior management to address the problem itself. Catalyst has heard time and again from executives that they need to know what action they can take. The more options you can provide, the more prepared management will be to do something useful. And you're much likelier to get what you want if you ask for it than if you wait and hope that busy managers will figure it out for themselves!

We have sponsored several seminars on flexible work options. Some have been for management, to provide information on what to do if an employee asks for such options.

—*Women's network leader*

We have a lot of policies on paper, but they're implemented poorly. And there is very little knowledge about whether those policies exist. So we wrote a letter to the company newspaper and tried to take a very nonconfrontational approach, but saying that it was wonderful that we were recognized in the *Working Mother* list of best companies, but that our policies need to be implemented better. That got a very good response. Now we're working on a letter to management about the upcoming rightsizing and how diversity needs to be addressed as part of those decisions and not put off until later.

—*Women's network leader*

The second category of advice entails identifying barriers facing women and recommending solutions. As you can imagine, this encompasses a wide range of *topics* and *activities.*

Topics can include

- Recruitment of women
- Advancement patterns of women compared to those of men
- Succession planning approaches
- Need for assistance with caregiving responsibilities
- Flexible work options
- Turnover rates among women compared to those among men
- Inhospitable work environments
- Movement of women from staff to line positions

What to Do?

Here's a quick reference list of some of the most effective advisory activities:

Educating Management

- Meet regularly with executive team to report back on issues facing women
- Create a "snapshot" of women in the company—a visual summary of women's progress as well as barriers still faced
- Invite executives from other companies (competitors or best practice companies) to address management on the importance of addressing gender issues and their strategies
- Design a checklist of actions executives can take to support women in their organization
- Communicate frequently with your management liaison and champions and provide information to help those individuals educate their colleagues

Identifying Barriers and Recommending Solutions

- Complete a climate survey on the environment for women
- Review studies and surveys from HR on related issues
- Assist the company in recruiting women
- Participate in the organization's diversity council
- Review career development systems and identify factors hindering women's success
- Examine personnel policies for possible negative impact on women
- Conduct a benchmarking study
- Examine flexibility needs of women and recommend solutions
- Pilot career development programs within the network

Activities can include

- Analysis of HR data
- Interviews with women at various levels
- Benchmarking company practices against competitors and best practices
- Assisting HR in designing programs
- Helping HR to understand the impact of policies as they are implemented

- Evaluating company programs and practices
- Presenting recommendations to management and HR
- Advising the company on long-term implementation

Most of the topics revolve around the career stages of women in the company and the environment in which they work. The activities center on gathering information, identifying issues, evaluating company responses, and recommending solutions.

> The company organized a focus group to judge people's interest in child care. But the way the questions were designed skewed the results. It appeared that women weren't interested in having child care facilities. Human Resources came to us and said "this doesn't make sense," so we explained the problem to them.
>
> *—Women's network leader*

> Most of the committees have been doing research. A lot of benchmarking, particularly on upward mobility and training and development. We've been looking outside our organization and doing some comparative work. We also look inside the organization to tie in with our diversity effort.
>
> *—Women's network leader*

> They helped us implement a tracking system for high-potential women, developed a program in sensitivity training, and helped us produce a "how to" booklet for taking advantage of our flexible hours policy.
>
> *—Management liaison*

Success Factors

A network's advisory role is unique. Doing it well requires different skills, strategies, and approaches than those demanded by other activities. In most other activities you are creating a participatory program or event. When you advise, others create the program or response. *The art of making the case for an issue and persuading others to act becomes critical.* Because of the differences in purpose and outcomes, success factors for these types of activities also differ.

Earlier in this section, we highlighted some factors to consider as you chose your advisory activities. These factors included meeting the needs of women, ensuring clear results, building credibility for the network, linking to management interest, and leveraging HR's expertise and accountability. You'll see that many of the same messages flow through the success factors.

Working at the Individual Level: Translating Corporate Career Development Systems into Strategies for Members

Career development activities mesh with your role of advising management and HR. For example, you may be focused on increasing the numbers of women in operations. To achieve that goal, actions must be taken at a number of different levels. Executives must make the issue a priority; HR must design systems that measure women's movement into line positions; numerical goals can be created to promote progress; managers must be held accountable. At the same time, women themselves need to be prepared to move into those positions. It is in this last area that women's networks can be most effective.

Rather than trying to design the systems or create the numerical goals that will move women into those spots, networks can work with women individually to prepare them for a lateral move or advancement. Some networks focusing on this issue have created mentoring programs that match women already in operations with women thinking of moving to that area. Other networks bring in outside speakers to educate women on the skills and experiences necessary. In that way, a network becomes an integral part of a strategy without getting involved in creation of systems or programs. A women's network can advise HR on the systems they create, but it shouldn't try to create them for itself. Instead, focus on translating HR strategies down to the level of individual women. Working at the individual level reinforces the different accountabilities for the network, HR, and management.

Make the Business Case to Take Action. The most important skill you need in advising management and HR is the ability to make the case for action. Once you've identified a need or problem, your job is to persuade executives and HR staff to help you in constructing a solution. To do that, you have three tasks.

The first is to *clearly document the challenge or need women face.* As noted earlier, numbers tell the best story. If you want to create a program for high-potential women in the organization, find statistics and data that best support your claim. Look for data showing that high-potential women plateau or leave the organization. Also look for qualitative data to help paint the picture. Conduct interviews or surveys to better understand the issues facing women in this group. The stronger the data you present, the more clearly executives and HR will hear your message.

The second task is to *sell the importance of addressing the issue.* Again, if you can find numbers that reinforce the negative impact this problem is having on the organization, your argument will be more persuasive. Ideally, you'd also like to have some more positive numbers that show the impact of addressing this issue. This information may have to come from outside your company. You can gather examples from competitors who have addressed the issue. Just as you made the business case for having a women's network, you need to make and sell the business case here.

Finally, the third activity is to *make it easier for executives and HR staff to take action*. Be prepared with solutions. Once you've shown that a barrier exists for women, show how that barrier can be removed. Try to highlight what management can do to address the issue, what HR can do, and what the women's network will do to support them. Reinforce the concept of partnership and create the detailed information allowing leaders and HR professionals to move forward with strategies.

Be Clear About Your Level of Involvement. Even at the earliest stages of your advisory role, you need to define your involvement. The concept of *intensity* that we described in the networking section also applies here. You can choose to have a lower level of involvement in advising management. For example, many networks sit on diversity councils or other representative groups. You are still advising the company on strategies related to women, but in a much less involved way. The impact is more diffuse, but this can be a more realistic option for groups with less time available. It is also a better option for groups with less support from HR or management. These groups also spend more time on education activities rather than recommending and implementing strategies. They need to build support among executives and thus their education role is a way to increase that support and credibility among senior managers.

Networks with more time and commitment from leaders and HR can provide more focused and involved advice. However, it is still essential to be realistic and clear about how much time and energy you can spend in this area. Conducting a benchmarking study or evaluating the feasibility of a child care center requires a great deal of work. Again, the payoffs may be larger, but only if you have the time, people, and ability to create a high-quality and well-researched product. Not giving it the necessary time and attention can backfire—presenting an ineffective analysis is certain to reduce the network's credibility.

Ensure the Program Achieves Its Measurable Objective. All network programs need specific and measurable objectives. Your advisory activities are the same as your career development activities in this area. If your focus is to educate management this year, set specific objectives about what information you need to convey, what vehicles you want to use, and what audiences you need to reach. All of these are easily evaluated. Evaluating whether the message has been heard and the commitment generated is more difficult. Recognize that changing attitudes and behaviors takes time and can often be beyond your control. However, you *can* control the message and how it's sent.

If your focus is gathering data or analyzing the environment for women, the evaluation process is clearly more straightforward. The same applies for the programs you recommend or pilot. If you're addressing low numbers of women accepting offers at the company, create a program for the network that addresses acceptance factors and set goals for increased acceptances among women. If you're creating a mentoring program, set objectives for junior and senior participants and evaluate whether those were met.

Checklist

☐ Create events linked to the network's mission and goals and designed to respond to members' interests and needs.

☐ Design activities with achievable goals.

☐ Effectively publicize each event and its purpose.

☐ Approach senior management and involve them as appropriate.

☐ Use strong evaluation tools to measure program impact.

GROWING FROM THE GRASS ROOTS: 3M

Origins. The committee began in 1975 as the Women's Advisory Council (WAC), a grassroots effort by women at 3M to explore the concerns of women employees. By 1978, the committee's role was formalized into a partnership with HR, where it became a subcommittee of the HR Advancement Committee. In 1985, it became the Women's Advisory Committee.

Support. From the beginning, WAC had strong support from HR. Support and respect of middle management has increased gradually. WAC members credit the respect and support they have now to their decision to partner with the company, as opposed to taking an adversarial role.

Membership. Committee membership is by application only, with twenty-five to thirty-five women of diverse backgrounds from all levels and functions selected each year. There are four subcommittees—strategic events planning, communications, issues, and membership. Membership and cochairs rotate every three years.

Leadership. Each year WAC convenes a "Let's Talk Issues" meeting. It conducts surveys and works with other diversity groups to find out which issues are of greatest interest to employees. That list is then ranked in regard to what WAC can do to address each issue, according to the best use of members' time and resources. WAC then creates an action plan for each of the top issues and selects two or three as priority goals.

Goals. In 1975 the founders of the group set out to explore the concerns of women employees with respect to employment opportunities, career advancement, and working conditions. In 1989 the group's mission was rephrased as an effort to eliminate gender-related barriers so as to achieve the full and equal participation of all employees working for the growth and success of 3M. In 1998, WAC aims to provide women's perspectives on workplace issues and help create an environment where all employees can contribute fully to the success of 3M.

Activities and Programs. In addition to researching current issues and making policy recommendations to the corporation, the group runs programs, some fea-

turing senior women executives and women board members, others on external topics of interest such as Minnesota history or individual development. In 1981 the committee launched its series of "Let's Talk Business" dinners to make known the opportunities available for all employees at 3M.

Communications. WAC's communications committee publicizes events everywhere—on tent cards in the cafeteria, e-mail lists, notices in the corporate newsletter, postings in hallways, noontime discussions on WAC open to all employees, and an intranet site called "The Frontier."

Advisory Role. WAC has a direct link to policymakers. 3M management, up to the top EVPs in the company, has been very receptive to the committee's recommendations and priorities.

CHAPTER SIX

STAY FOCUSED!
KEEPING ON TRACK AS THE NETWORK AGES

Guiding Question: How can the network maintain its effectiveness and membership commitment over time?

One could say that a network's life over the long haul depends, basically, on three things: membership, leadership, and a fair amount of hard work. Money helps, too. This chapter provides a guide to the day-to-day business of running a network, largely through answers to the questions that women ask Catalyst most often on the subject. Here, too, you will learn that it is entirely possible to keep a network up and growing smoothly despite any setbacks it may encounter along the way and without overburdening any of its leaders, members, or supporters.

One concern that women involved in networks share frequently with Catalyst is the loss of momentum they experience after the first few years. That's not too surprising. A new network receives a great deal of attention. Getting the network up and running requires a tremendous amount of time and effort. After the first few years, both the attention from others and the intense involvement of members often wane. Nevertheless, some women's networks have been in existence for more than twenty years. 3M's Women's Advisory Council recently celebrated its twentieth anniversary. Hoffman-LaRoche's women's network has been in place since the late '70s. Clearly, it is possible to sustain a network over time.

After the initial high-intensity, high-energy period, a network needs to begin paying even closer attention to its current membership and to concentrate on bringing in new members. A membership that is diverse, committed, and replenished regularly is one of the most important ingredients for a successful network. This

chapter outlines some well-tested strategies designed to keep the membership interested and involved and to continually bring new members into the fold.

The period after that first rush of activity is also the time to evaluate what
you've accomplished and to check whether the mission and goals of the network
are still on target. By keeping focused on the alignment between the network's
goals and activities, you can avoid the "mission drift" that networks sometimes experience.

Now you can start thinking, too, about how to broaden your reach to include
groups outside of the network. In this chapter, we will focus primarily on building
ties to other employee networks in your company and reaching out to women who
are not members of the network. Cementing relationships with both these groups
requires consensus building and shared goals, but can ultimately lead to important partnerships.

Basic Housekeeping

This first section of the chapter covers the basics of keeping a network going. Here
we offer some simple organizational strategies for keeping the network on track:

- Running effective meetings
- Ensuring leadership succession
- Asking for and getting money

Membership Meetings

Q: Our meetings don't run very smoothly. Either not enough people attend
to make it worth our time, or so many people come that it becomes unwieldy. How can we improve the meetings so we get the work done and get
to know each other at the same time?

A: This brings up an important dual purpose to most network meetings.
Clearly, you meet as a group to make decisions, communicate progress, and
agree upon next steps. However, you also want to meet the other members.
To accomplish these two goals takes careful planning.

If too few people are attending the meetings, that may mean you're having too
many meetings. Many networks that originally had standing monthly meetings
now meet every two months or even once a quarter. A drop in participation made
leaders realize that they didn't need a meeting every four weeks. This also allowed
more work to be done in between meetings by committees. Low numbers of mem-

bers at meetings can also be a symptom of a larger problem. Perhaps it's time to look at your goals and mission. Are they still responding to members' needs? Or are members so overwhelmed with job commitments that they can't devote as much time to the network as they once did?

> The network's work came out of people's nights and weekends. That is, I think, one of the pervasive problems.
>
> —*Management liaison*

If members have had to reduce the amount of time they devote to the network, consider scaling back activities for the time being. Reduce the meetings and reduce the events, and make really sure that what remains is interesting and important to members.

Managing meetings is almost a science. A designated leader is essential to make a meeting work and keep everyone on track. Some networks rotate this leadership position, others have the network leader take charge of all network meetings. What follows are some strategies for making your meetings both efficient and effective.

- *Start meetings promptly and end on time.* There's nothing more frustrating than meetings that start late—and then usually also end later than expected. For efficiency, make sure your meetings don't last any longer than necessary for the work to be done.
- *Create a clear, written agenda.* A formal agenda is almost the only way for meetings to proceed as promised. Be sure to include committee updates, upcoming activities, discussion of new ideas, and networking time in your agendas. Many networks hold meetings around lunchtime so members can spend part of the time eating together and having informal conversations.
- *Have participants identify themselves.* As members speak, be sure to ask them to say who they are. Some networks have a "getting to know you" period during meetings with new members.
- *Keep the meeting focused, positive, and action-oriented.* Especially if you have fewer meetings, it can be tempting to go off on tangents. Leaders often complain of members spending too much time discussing company gossip or problems in the workplace. Such problems do need to be discussed, but you should parcel out time specifically for that. Keep the business section of the meeting focused on updates and decisions and reserve time at the end of the meeting or at another time to discuss more general issues.
- *Respond to the needs of women in different locations and with different work schedules.* Many networks have members in various offices and regions, as well as some who don't work a traditional nine-to-five schedule. It's important to vary the location and time

of the meeting so as many people as possible can attend. One network rotates its meetings among the three office locations to increase participation. Another regularly holds conference calls to update a geographically dispersed leadership team.

Elections and Leadership Succession

Q: The leadership team we created at the start of our network is ready to step down. How can we motivate women to run for these leadership positions and what sort of process do we need to organize the elections themselves?

A: Leadership succession is a crucial issue. Having a core group of initiators who run the network for its first few years is invaluable. This consistency in leadership helps build a strong base of support and systems. However, it is equally critical to pass that leadership to a new group of women.

There is a range of options for leadership structures. Whether you have a single leader, a pair of coleaders, or a triumvirate at the top, you need to start developing the next generation early. Look for members who have taken smaller roles in heading up committees or organizing events and consider them for future leadership positions. Speak with them directly about their interests and encourage them to take on more visible roles within the network.

We have elections in November each year for the following year. The president, vice president, and all the other chairs come up with names of people we think might be interested. They may not know what they want to do but by talking to them and finding out where their interests lie, we can see if we could find a spot for them.

—*Women's network leader*

Most members need some encouragement to take on leadership positions. Likewise, long-term leaders may need encouragement to let go. Someone who has created a network and seen it though its infancy can find it difficult to pass on the leadership mantle. While this situation can be problematic to address, it is absolutely necessary that you do so. Otherwise you could end up with a network going nowhere but downhill. Once the entrenched leader steps down, though, be sure to continue to involve her—perhaps as an adviser. She has a wealth of knowledge that future leaders will want to access. Women's networks sometimes have a formal board of directors; past leaders are often members.

The elections themselves are straightforward administrative processes. For smaller networks, there may not be a formal election at all. If all the most interested people can fit in one room and find the time to do so, it's enough to get together and talk over the question of next year's leadership. Members volunteer, and depending on how many spots are available, it can be a decision made at that very meeting. Larger networks often use a formal election process with nominations, summaries of each candidate's qualifications sent out by paper or electronic mail, and votes taken on a set date. It is important to keep an eye on the group's real size so you will recognize when it has grown too large for the informal process.

> At the annual meeting people can nominate themselves or others who want to run for Board of Directors positions. Then they put a little summary of their experience, why they want to run, and what they want to accomplish on e-mail. It all goes out and members vote for those people they want to represent them on the Board.
>
> *—Women's network leader*

Some success strategies for leadership succession and elections:

- Create a formal process to nominate potential leaders.
- Have clearly defined lengths of term for all leadership positions.
- Overlap newly elected leaders with previous leaders to ensure continuity and the sharing of information.
- Work toward diversity in nominations to ensure diversity in the leadership of the network.

This last point is especially important. The women leading the network should reflect the demographics of the membership and also include members who reflect the locations, levels, and functions of members. If your membership represents corporate and manufacturing sites, be sure to include people from both those areas in the leadership team. Carve out roles for senior women to play, either as leaders or as advisers.

Funding

Q: So far, we've been holding events that don't cost money. However, we want to bring in a speaker this year and have an off-site event for members. Both of these require funds that we don't have. Should we get a budget from HR? Should we charge dues? What are the benefits and drawbacks of each?

A: It doesn't take long for a network to need money. Both the budget and the dues options have pros and cons.

Accepting a Budget. Fifty-one percent of networks surveyed by Catalyst have a budget given to them by the company. They often work with Human Resources to project their budgetary needs for the year and can rely on that money being available. Being funded by HR also lends a certain credence to the network throughout the company. It reinforces the importance of the network and its activities.

> I think there's a real advantage to having funding from the company. Not just with money issues, but because every time there's a budget discussion, when policy is being made, then there's a discussion of the value of the women's group. I spoke to our CFO about that and he said, "You're absolutely right."
>
> *—Women's network leader*

Other Options. However, not all networks can gain funding from the organization. In that case, many groups charge dues for all members. (See survey for more information.) Some networks believe that charging dues results in a more committed membership. Another option is to charge nonmembers for the events the network organizes.

> We do have a membership fee and that supports some of the events. We do charge nonmembers, I think it's $5, if they come to an event. What we really try to do is get them to join, but if they don't want to join we charge them for the event.
>
> *—Women's network leader*

Some networks are able to gain access to outside funding through professional associations or local groups. This occurs more rarely, but can be done in areas where there are many active women-focused groups in the community. Finally, some networks receive funding from the organization, but need to charge dues as well to carry out their programs.

Membership

One of the most common questions women's networks have is how to keep the entire membership involved in the activities of the network. There is a big difference in commitment between the members who keep the network going and those who simply attend events.

> We're about two years old, and the problem we're experiencing is that there's a very small group of women who are very active and very dedicated. Our events

are well attended, we get a lot of people, but we have problems getting people to help.

—Women's network leader

Our biggest issue right now is just can we survive. We have a very small, very interested group of people who do it on their own and they're burnt to a crisp. We're just trying to figure out how we can entice people to be members, and not just come and listen to a speaker once a month.

—Women's network leader

Keeping the membership committed and building the membership is a challenging task. It's also work that many networks must do constantly. In this section, we will be answering some of the most frequently asked questions in these areas, and offering strategies to assist you in these efforts.

Increasing the Leadership Pool

Q: We have a large group of women who've indicated interest in the network. How can we translate that into more committee leaders or members who take charge of activities?

A: In most networks, there is a group of women who aren't leaders yet, but are more active than the general membership. It is this group that you want to target as you search for team leaders. As you try to move these members from participants in events to organizers, it's important to capitalize on their interests and stress the benefits of leadership.

Capitalizing on Potential Leaders' Interests. Members usually have one or two key areas they are interested in. As a current leader, your job is to help members figure out ways to work on their own goals and support the network in the process. If someone is interested in community events, reach out to her and suggest some options. Start small, so the work isn't overwhelming, as a way to introduce the member to leadership roles. As she becomes more comfortable with these activities, she'll be more likely to take on future organizing positions.

I think the one-to-one personal touch really is what's most effective for getting participation in the network. . . . I think if you really talk to people, sit down, have lunch with them, say the exact things you would in a letter, that seems to get people over the hump from inaction to action.

—Women's network leader

Stressing the Benefits. Whether it is gaining skills, fulfilling personal goals, or connecting with management, there are clear gains for those who take a more active role. Try to convey what you personally have gotten out of a leadership role. Members who can see the direct benefits of a new position are more likely to take it on. Also consider making leadership positions team-based. Moving from a participant to an organizer is an easier jump if you're doing it with someone else. Try matching up first-time leaders with more experienced advisers. Remember that the more successful people's first attempts at leadership are, the more likely they are to continue with it.

Finally, recognize that all members' participation will vary over time. Try to reach out to as many potential leaders as you can. But if someone can't get more involved at the moment, be understanding and come back to them when they have more time.

> We've been careful in terms of keeping people involved to absolutely refuse to guilt anybody about their participation. When someone says they're too busy right now to be involved, we say thanks for what you've done and we go find somebody else who's got some energy that quarter or that six months.
>
> —*Women's network leader*

Maintaining a Cohesive and Inclusive Network

Q: Our network is open to all women at the company. It's important for us to have that level of inclusion, but the group is becoming unwieldy because inevitably there are subgroups with different goals. How can we sustain our cohesion, yet still address the more specific goals of these subgroups?

A: For all-inclusive groups, it's a balancing act between meeting the needs of the membership as a whole and meeting the needs of various member populations. While it may seem difficult to address these two sets of needs, there are some clear strategies you can use.

• *Identify groupwide needs and individual population needs.* Women's networks often create two sets of goals. There are the goals that address the interests of all members—personal effectiveness activities, for instance, such as speakers or career development seminars. The second set of goals is specific to the groups within the network. To identify those goals, you need to first figure out the clearest groupings of women within the network. These may be based on location, function, level, or other determinants.

Once you've identified the groups and learned their specific goals, create your annual plan for the network including items from both lists. Use the same

Working Together: Team-Building Phases

Successful groups recognize that it is important to spend time on team-building activities not only when the group is forming but also throughout the life of the network. Developing an atmosphere of trust and candor takes time and effort, but it's well worth it. Once you've built a cohesive team, your own efficiency and effectiveness grow tremendously. No matter whether the group is doing well or struggling, it's important to pay attention to internal group dynamics.

Women's networks commonly pass through these stages:

Forming: When women first come together to explore the possibility of a network, usually there is a range of attitudes about the idea. Some women are excited about the concept and are optimistic regarding the impact the group can have for women in their organization. Others are skeptical and express concerns about how the group will be perceived by other employees or by management. Finally, there may be some women who are guardedly optimistic and form a tentative attachment to the group.

It is important, therefore, to spend some time building a shared purpose among the members. You've already devoted time to getting acquainted with one another and determining the group's purpose. Now, you must also establish ways of working together. Defining ground rules for group discussion and communications is especially critical because all network members have responsibilities and allegiances not only to the network itself but to the department or function in which they work.

The ground rules basically are very simple. What's said there stays there. All conversations are considered confidential. Take sexual harassment issues, for example. A member who is a lawyer or works for the EEO department has to put on her professional hat. So the rule is, "If you feel your professional role is [affecting what you bring to the discussion] you have to say so." We try to stay away from those issues.

—*Women's network leader*

Storming: During this period, members may start to experience anxiety as they realize the amount of work needed to accomplish their goals. During this stage, there may be sharp fluctuations in members' attitudes about the group and its ability to be successful. Members may still be trying to rely solely on their personal and professional experience, resisting any need for collaborating with other group members.

This is a critical stage in the development of a cohesive team. These questions may help you figure out what's wrong and improve the effectiveness of your group:

- Does the group rely on one person to keep the discussion going?
- Are people repeating points, unsure of whether anyone heard them the first time?
- Are discussions stuck? Is there an inability to let go of one topic and move onto the next?
- Are there clear subgroups or "lone wolves" in the meetings who are reducing the effectiveness of the group?
- Is there a lack of interest on the part of members or groups of members in what the group is doing?
- Do members display a negative attitude toward change, people, and team building in general?
- Can opposing views or negative feelings be expressed without fear of punishment?
- Are discussions in the hallway after the meeting freer and more candid than those that take place during the meeting?

Norming: During this third stage, members begin to set aside personal needs or agendas and start to work together as a team. Group members will begin to be able to express criticism constructively. They will, therefore, have more time and energy to devote to working on group goals.

> There definitely has to be a strong commitment and somehow you grow that. It doesn't happen immediately. We found that we really had to build up a level of trust where people could relax and be themselves. It takes a while to develop that.

> —*Women's network leader*

Performing: In the last stage of team growth members have become more comfortable with each other. They understand the group's purpose better. They know what is expected of them. Group members have begun to exhibit an ability to prevent problems before they occur or constructively address them when they do. They form a stronger attachment to the group; the group's activities usually become more effective.

Most women's networks experience cycles with regard to teams. Leaders of established women's groups describe varying patterns of participation and enthusiasm for group activities over the years. These cycles are influenced by a number of factors. Lack of progress on a project or activity may undermine members' enthusiasm. Success with a particular issue, especially one of great importance to the group, will of course have the reverse effect—interest and excitement are likely to increase.

These cycles are also influenced by the resistance or encouragement the group receives from management and by issues that affect the company as a whole, such as downsizing or reengineering. Members become focused on holding on to their jobs and may have less time and energy to devote to group activities. Interestingly, some networks have used those instances to increase participation, by responding to the challenges:

> All of a sudden my membership is very high because we've been putting on a number of programs that address current [downsizing] issues in the corporation. If people start feeling that they need a network and they need support you'll find that membership increases.
>
> *—Women's network leader*

Successful networks recognize that team building is a continual process, especially during a leadership transition.

> We have what we call a transition in January each year. And the most effective meetings have been those that are very much internally focused. So we do some initial team-building skills, and we do some initial strategic planning for the year.
>
> *—Women's network leader*

priority-setting approach you've used before to set your agenda. You may not be able to address every group's goals all at once, but once you know what they are, you can build them into the long-term plans of the network.

> For a specified period the focus will be on technical women and their career development. In another period it will be breaking that barrier from nonexempt to exempt, or child care issues, or whatever. We give ourselves the openness and the option to work in any direction, but focus on one or two things at a time.
>
> *—Women's network leader*

• *Consider forming subteams specific to these populations.* Depending on how large your network is, you may want to create subteams to focus on issues specific to each subgroup. Networks have created subteams for women in technical positions, in field locations, or in various pay or position levels. Be careful, though, to maintain the strength of the network as a whole. Otherwise, the group itself can weaken. Always work to balance the needs of the individuals with the needs of the group.

Membership Perks

Q: To reward current members, we would like to create some membership perks. What have other networks done in this area?

A: Many networks do add tangible items to what might be the less immediately obvious benefits of joining a network. These can include memberships in professional groups, discounts on magazines, free admission to local events, or other passes or options. Some networks create work-related items such as pens or pads of paper emblazoned with the group's name and symbol—things that members enjoy having and that help publicize the group at the same time.

We're looking at membership pins which would have the year that you joined, with a diamond chip for the founding members and a sapphire for the five-year members. I think that would be marvelous if that became part of your office dress, this pin, in the sense of gaining acceptance and a real presence within the organization.

—Women's network leader

Another benefit of membership is being able to attend exclusive events. Putting on an activity or reception just for network members can be a real reward. Of course, if these events include access to senior managers, the group and membership in it becomes that much more prestigious.

We've initiated a series of cocktail receptions with senior executives. We started with [the president] who was brand new, and we had him first, before anybody else in the company did. He spent two hours taking questions and was the last to leave. To come and talk one-on-one with him you had to be a member. We've try to position these receptions as premiums or perks for membership.

—Women's network leader

Recognizing Your Successes

Q: The network has achieved a great deal in the last few years. How can we recognize everyone who has helped and publicize our accomplishments?

A: We can't say this enough—*take time to celebrate your successes!* Whether it is a small or large victory, be sure to recognize what you've accomplished and let others know about it. Internally, highlight the members who were the leaders and doers. Externally, publicize the success of your group through as many channels as you can find.

But don't stop at network successes. Many networks also highlight successful women in their company. One network sends out an award each time a woman is promoted to a senior position, congratulating her and letting her know the network is behind her. The Honeywell women's network has a formal award for managers who develop and promote women. This not only increases the visibility of the men and women championing women's advancement, but also links these critical individuals with the network.

Building the Membership

Membership has ebbed and flowed. We've gone from a combined membership of 300 down to around 150. Now we're back up to 250. For those of you who have been involved or will be involved as leaders, you'll see that as issues become hot, participation will rise.

—Women's network leader

Successful networks use a range of strategies to gain membership throughout the life of the network. These networks think not only in terms of sheer numbers, but also about whether the membership has the right mix of women from a range of levels and is racially diverse.

Increasing Membership

Q: Our membership has leveled off and we're trying to attract new members. What are some of our options?

A: You can use a range of different strategies to increase your membership. One way is to think about potential members as belonging to one of three groups. Reaching out to each group requires a different approach.

• *Women who know little about the network and have never been involved with the group.* This is the largest group of potential members and the most dispersed. Thus connecting with them takes larger events or mailings. Some networks have formal "meet the network" events annually, open to all potential members in the organization and publicized through direct invitations and announcements via e-mail and newsletters. These events often have two objectives: to convey information about the network itself and why participants should join—perhaps in the form of a presentation by the network leader—and at the same time to give a sample of what the network does, maybe by including a career development speaker at the event.

If you're organizing an event like this, be sure to create opportunities for participants to join right then and there. Following up with them after the event takes a great deal more time and effort on the network's part.

• *Women who may know about the group through colleagues or friends who are members.* To best tap into this group, you'll want to reach out to people individually. They already have an understanding of the network's mission and goals, so the more general events are less effective. Ask members to speak directly with these potential members about their interest in joining the group. Some networks have membership drives and expect that each member will bring in three to five additional participants. Using this approach is very effective because the membership message can be tailored individually. Also, because new members are joining a group where they already know participants, the orientation process can be easier and can result in a more cohesive group. Relying only on this strategy can result in a somewhat insular group, however, so balance the approach with outreach strategies targeting groups of women who have historically not been members of the network.

• *Former members who have decided not to renew their membership.* This is an important category, whether or not any of the people you approach decide to join again. It can be a bellwether for how the network is fulfilling the needs of its members. Understanding the reasons former members decided not to renew their membership and what the network could do to respond to those reasons is important information you can get from no one else.

> We have a membership drive every June, then we wait a month, then we have the location coordinators [in the different buildings] send e-mail to the people who haven't renewed to remind them about renewing. Then, two months later, we send whoever hasn't renewed a couple of questions, asking them to share the reasons they decided not to continue and whether there are any suggestions they have to make this an organization they would join.
>
> —*Women's network leader*

Once you have signed up new members, you need an orientation strategy. It's important to convey to them the history of the network, its current goals and strategies, and the inner workings of the group. It's equally important to hear their ideas and interests. New members can eventually make a difference in the group's tone and approach. Be flexible and try to balance the need to ensure continuity within the group with the imperative of change.

> At least one-third of the members are new within the last two years, so they don't understand how isolated it was before, and they don't understand the needs of the group as well as some of the older women do.
>
> —*Women's network leader*

Divisiveness is making us lose power and I think it's because our group has been around for a long time. The women who are involved now didn't formulate the goals themselves. You don't want to say to anybody, "You don't think like we do, we don't want you." Here are people willing to be active and involved, you don't say to them "go away."

—Women's network leader

No matter how old the network may be, it's important to integrate new members into it. If you have a small group of new members, you can have a formal orientation session. Many larger networks use a new members' kit, which should include these materials:

- Mission statement
- Network history or timeline of major accomplishments and activities
- Summary of network's operating rules and structure
- Names and numbers of steering committee members and committee chairs
- Announcement of upcoming activities
- Application for network directories
- Information on how to join subcommittees

Including Senior Women

Q: We're having problems involving senior women in our network. Some are too busy; others feel it's too risky to be members. What can we do to include them in events and leverage their expertise and experience?

A: It's important to have senior women involved with the group. They have experience in the company that is invaluable to members, knowledge to share about career success strategies, and important contacts among senior leaders. The solution is to involve senior women where their skills, experiences, contacts, and backgrounds are most needed, shaping your appeals on an individual basis tailored to their own needs for development and recognition.

Often it's difficult to get the most senior women to participate. Networks need to reach out one-to-one to these very senior women and give them specific things to do.

—Management liaison

The approach is similar to that used for gaining executive feedback during the climate survey. However, before you turn to your senior female colleagues, first identify where you need their help. Is it as internal advisers for the network? Then invite them to join an executive advisory team assisting the network leaders. Would you like to have them act as career coaches or share their success strategies for advancement? Then ask them to participate in a mentoring program or on a panel of executive women. Do you need them to be your executive champions with senior leaders in the company? Then approach them with that need. The key is to be as specific as possible and give them as much help as possible.

> We have really got the support of our women officers and we try to involve them every step of the way. We always make sure that at a steering meeting we have a woman officer. We have two women officers assigned to our subcommittees, and although they can't come to all of the meetings, the chair coordinates back and forth with them. We don't have mechanisms to get to our top management directly, but we can get to them indirectly through our women officers.
>
> —*Women's network leader*

It's also important to understand how the network can respond to the senior women's specific needs, which can be dramatically different from those of the membership as a whole.

> We recently had a two-day, off-site executive women's meeting. What came up were issues that never come up at the lower levels of management women. Totally different issues relating to business and communications.
>
> —*Women's network leader*

As you do with the other populations within the group, design activities that target senior women's participation. Often these are networking-centered and include senior women and higher-level executives. Other options include outside speakers or external training and development opportunities for executive women.

Ensuring a Diverse Membership

Q: We look at our membership and we are not a racially diverse group. How can we better understand why women of color aren't joining as members and what we can do to make our group a more diverse one?

A: Many of the network leaders who participated in the Catalyst study were concerned about the lack of ethnic and racial diversity in their groups. Some conceded they had not made enough of an effort to recruit women of color. Others who had investigated this issue often found that women of color saw the network as addressing issues that were not relevant to them, and felt that issues specific to women of color were not being raised within the network.

> We are being perceived as the white women's group . . . we have had women of
> color in the network but they haven't felt their issues have gotten much attention.
>
> —*Women's network leader*

Women's networks that have been successful in creating a racially and eth-
nically diverse membership have done two things. First, they have examined their
network for biases that may be in place or approaches that discourage women of
color from joining. They look at not only the internal systems but also at the events
themselves. Were their speakers and panelists at events diverse? Did their exhibits
for Women's History Month reflect the experiences of women of color? Had they
connected with outside experts on women of color in organizations? Answers to
these questions helped them better understand what prevented women of color
from joining the network.

The second strategy is to take an active role in recruiting women of color. As
in other recruiting efforts, women's networks surveyed or interviewed potential
members who are women of color to better understand their needs and interests.
They then used that information to create appropriate programs and activities.
Where there are other employee networks targeted to people of color, women's
networks partner with those groups in recruitment efforts.

> Two and a half years ago, we realized that our diversity was nonexistent. We
> have large Asian, African American, and Hispanic populations, but we didn't
> see those names popping up on our membership lists. So we did a benchmark
> study when we sent out the yearly renewal form to ask a few questions and then
> we set goals. We made sure our programs and speakers were diverse and that
> the topics were of interest to all women. For example, we had a speaker from a
> local university talk about the research she had done on success strategies for
> Korean American women. That brought us a lot of members.
>
> —*Women's network leader*

Connecting with Other Employee Networks

Q: There are other employee networks at our company. I'd like to link up with
them so we can coordinate our events and advisory roles to management.
How should we go about doing that?

A: Any network can be more efficient if it partners with the other employee
groups in the organization. There are many shared issues and strategies
across groups and you can help each other with events and learn from each
other.

Network of Networks—Kimberly-Clark

Kimberly-Clark's Network of Networks is an effective example of one approach to this issue. KC has eight employee networks, four of which were launched at one time—for African Americans, Asians, gays and lesbians, and women. The original four have since been joined by an Eastern European network, a Hispanic network, an adult dependent care network, and NEON, a network for new employees.

In 1994, the firm had grassroots employee groups; they were neither formal nor championed by the corporation. HR brought members of these groups together to talk about the benefits of formal networks. Then HR convened a "come and consider" meeting of all women employees at the operations headquarters (the work site of about five thousand employees), at which Bickley Townsend of Catalyst spoke on the benefits of women's networks. HR recorded that presentation and circulated it to other sites to help them get started.

Next, HR created an employee committee to create guidelines and structures for all the networks, which then communicated with each other through a Joint Network Council. There is also a subcommittee of the corporate steering committee to support the networks. The networks are standardized in their relation to the company, each having a designated management sponsor or cosponsor and each with a designated leader or point person. While they continue to communicate through the council, they are relatively independent when it comes to their strategies for meeting their members' needs. The women's network, with six hundred members (including some men), is by far the largest.

Often, networks think about collaboration in the following three ways:

• *Partnering on events:* There are often overlaps among networks when it comes to events and programs. So it makes sense to pool your resources. Networks often cosponsor speakers or career development programs.

One of the most effective things that we are doing is that the women's council and the black employee network are combining efforts for a mentoring program. Because both groups believed that mentoring should be available to everybody at all levels of the organization, we joined forces. It's been a nice approach to working together on a common issue.

—Women's network leader

You can also help each other in recruiting organizers or volunteers for events. One women's network was having trouble getting volunteers for a particular event until a member of the black employee network asked how they were doing. He helped them sign up a number of people, and that helped to cement future partnerships between the two networks.

Most networks have limited financial resources. By combining forces, they can often create more effective events with larger agendas. At the same time, they set up links between individuals in the different groups, which are critical to ensuring future collaboration.

• *Creating a coalition to advise management and Human Resources:* The other area of overlap is the advisory role most networks play. This can be tricky, though, because while the roles overlap, the recommendations to executives often don't. Each employee network may have slightly different recommendations; coordinating them can be a difficult and very political process. When two networks are competing for management attention, for instance, working together can be challenging at best. However, networks that do link together to present common recommendations often end up with their suggestions being accepted.

At one company, the Women's Council compiled a list of goals for the company to become the employer of choice for women. They made a presentation to the Executive Committee of the company and won approval from senior management. Meanwhile, however, other employee groups had formed. The women's network realized problems would develop if they were to publish their list without consulting with other networks first, so they worked with them to create an all-encompassing list. Some items were reworked, others were consolidated. It took over a year, but by the end, the groups had formed a coalition and were able to present a new, unified list of goals to the senior management team.

• *Helping other networks get started.* Often a women's network is the first employee group at an organization. As other networks form, the women's network can be a resource to them. Many of the initial steps recommended in this book—identifying needs, building support, and creating internal systems—work equally well for other networks. Network leaders often meet with the organizers of other networks to share ideas and insight about structure and strategies.

There are a number of ways networks can work together to achieve their mutual goals and enhance their effectiveness. Partnerships often take time to build, so think about small ways to collaborate if you're just beginning. Ask for a list of upcoming events from other networks and include those events in your newsletter. Try setting up a regular meeting among employee network leaders, or creating a liaison who regularly checks in with other groups on your own and their progress. Once you're on a solid footing, you can branch out into more complex collaboration.

Building a Coalition

When groups join together to achieve common goals, they create a coalition. Coalitions share certain characteristics, success factors, and sources of conflict.

Characteristics:

- Coalitions are usually built around a specific purpose.
- Some of the goals and strategies of the various groups will not coincide.
- Working in coalition takes compromising and a lot of negotiating, but a coalition can extend your impact into areas you hadn't reached before.
- Members must be willing to discuss problems openly, listen closely, and give and receive criticism.
- Leave room for each group to accept, refuse, or modify suggestions.

Success Factors:

- Members of a coalition need to maintain their own identity and deal with each other on terms of equality and mutual respect.
- The self-interest of each group must be clear to its own membership. Its need for the broader base must also be recognized.
- The coalition goals must be seen as achievable. It's important to identify many short-term goals as well as longer-term activities.
- Members of a coalition must accept and value differences in priorities and styles.
- Anticipate conflict and try to handle it constructively.

Potential Sources of Conflict:

- Ambiguity in responsibility for roles.
- Actions developed by one of the coalition groups may not mesh with the others. Actions taken at different levels may be contradictory.
- Territorial claims. Conflict can erupt when one group sees another encroaching on its turf or damaging it by other activities.
- Pressure from the outside may drive a wedge between coalition partners.

Helping Other Women in the Company

Q: We are a small network and our membership does not include nonexempt women or those in the field. While we're not ready to expand our network to include those groups of women, we would still like to invite them to our events and help them. How can we do this?

A: Designing programs to respond to the interests of nonmembers can be tricky. On one hand, they are an important group within the corporation. On the other hand, they aren't officially members of the network and reaching out to them can reinforce the network's exclusivity. To minimize the potential backlash, consider the options discussed in this section for connecting with women outside your membership.

- *Encourage the formation of other targeted women's networks.* If your network does not want to expand its membership, consider helping other groups of women form their own networks. There are many networks for women engineers, women in sales, women in secretarial positions, women in field locations, and so on. Your network could act as an adviser during the early stages. Once a new network has formed, be sure to coordinate your efforts and share your resources.

- *Use your resources and support to meet their needs.* Rather than encouraging the creation of a separate network, some networks have identified the needs of different groups of women, worked to construct solutions, and presented their recommendations to management. Most often, this occurs when an executive women's network reaches out to more junior women. While the junior women aren't members, their interests can be brought to management by the more senior women.

  This strategy requires delicacy. If not managed carefully, the network can appear paternalistic or heavy-handed. Be careful about how you approach other groups of women and be certain they are looking for assistance. Don't try to provide help where none is wanted or needed.

- *Act as an informal resource.* An easy way to assist women who are not members is through the network's career resources. For example, some networks create libraries of information on women in the workplace. Others create summaries of training opportunities at the company. These can be made available to all employees. Publicize the existence of these resources throughout the company to ensure you're reaching the largest audience possible. If your network conducts companywide activities and promotes them in a newsletter, be sure the newsletter is posted in public areas.

- *Create larger events open to all women in the organization.* A final strategy is to include all women at the larger conferences or events you create. In so doing, recognize that their interests should be integrated into the program. For example, a conference for all women should address the needs of women in various functions, locations, and levels.

Evaluating the Network's Effectiveness

Q: Our network has been around for four years. We've done a great deal in those years and we want to reconnect with members to evaluate whether we're still fulfilling our mission. We also want to make sure we're on track with their needs. How can we do this?

A: The longer a network is in existence, the more important it becomes to evaluate whether the network is meeting its goals and responding to member interests. This goes beyond examining the effectiveness of a specific program. Instead, you're looking at the network as a whole—the activities, the tone, the approach, the strategies—and evaluating whether that still fits with your mission and your membership.

Consider the audiences you want to reach, the messages you want to send, and the results you want to see. Then examine your programs to see if those goals are being met.

We do some focus group work with the general members and bring the results of that back to the group. Then each one of the committees is going to look at those results and compare them with our mission and goals. First of all, we may find that some of our goals need to be expanded or changed somehow based on the input we get from our general members. The specific goals may be modified and from those goals will come specific actions that each committee will take over the next few years.

—Women's network leader

In some cases, networks create a specific task force to evaluate the satisfaction of members.

Right now we have a general membership task force in place that's asking the members, "What is it that you believe this group ought to be providing you with. What do you want, need, and expect to get as a member of the women's council. Where do you think the women's council is going?" Then we take that back to the steering committee.

—Women's network leader

A process like this is too comprehensive to be done annually. It's sufficient for a network to reexamine its impact and member commitment every three to five years, using a process similar to the initial climate survey. The tools for gaining member input and the process of assessing desired goals and outcomes work equally well here.

Common results of an evaluation include new or modified mission statements or goals, the creation of new task forces and the dissolution of others, and the adoption of new methods of outreach for new members. In most cases, the results involve tweaking the network to keep it on the right track. Doing this every few years ensures the long-term health of the network.

Checklist

☐ Create network processes that run smoothly, including membership meetings and leadership succession.

☐ Develop strategies to build membership and encourage members to take on leadership roles.

☐ Incorporate needs of member populations and overall membership into network goals and activities.

☐ Institute activities to reward members and celebrate network successes.

☐ Design orientation approach for new members.

☐ Examine membership for diversity and create strategies to address any barriers to participation by women of specific groups.

☐ Ensure participation of senior women.

☐ Partner with other networks.

☐ Create approach to evaluate overall network impact and member satisfaction.

CHAPTER SEVEN

WHAT IF YOU FACE REAL PROBLEMS?
HOW TO MAKE THEM
CONQUERABLE CHALLENGES

Guiding Question: How can the network recognize and respond to some of the major challenges and problems it might have to face?

Women's networks are continually adapting and making changes—modifying subcommittee goals, seeking to expand audiences, retargeting other efforts. Goals are rarely accomplished along a straight line; indeed, the line is usually full of kinks and turns. Being flexible allows you to adjust without changing the network as a whole.

Sometimes, however, more significant change is needed. This chapter is about those times. Circumstances may require a major decision related to the network, its mission, goals, and activities—up to and including shutting the whole thing down. Most women's networks have faced at least one such situation if they've been in existence for a few years.

Internal or external events may force a network to reevaluate itself. Internal changes are usually related to member needs or the needs of other women at the company. External events center on changes in management or organizational shifts. Guiding the network through these transitions requires flexibility and willingness to change.

Common Internal Challenges

- Notable drop-off in membership participation
- Concern over exclusivity of membership criteria
- Lack of accomplishments or inability to reach goals

- Significant changes in member interests
- Network leadership changes or resignations
- Fulfillment of short- and long-term goals with no clear future activities
- Large reduction in time commitment of members
- Assumption of network responsibilities by Human Resources

Common External Challenges

- Downsizing at company or business unit level
- Relocation of corporate or field locations
- Departure of executive champion to another organization or a different role
- Appointment of a less supportive executive team
- Gender-related litigation requiring network to take on a different role

In the face of any of these events, do two things. First, identify the problem, not just the symptoms. For example, say membership is dropping off. The natural response is to recruit more members. However, the real problem may be that the network's mission is out of sync with member interests. You need to address the problems of current members before you bring new members on board.

Second, construct an appropriate response. It's important to recognize what the network can and cannot do. If you're facing an economic downturn in your organization, you can't make much headway against the overarching fact of layoffs. However, you can create programs that address the specific needs of members and other employees during difficult times.

Be clear about what you're willing and able to do. If, for example, a group of members wants to change the membership criteria, then that's a significant decision and one that requires support from a majority of the membership. If you don't have that support, you'll end up with new criteria but a divided membership.

Many of these larger challenges or events can be answered by the same techniques already recommended for determining what a network needs to do and for building support for its activities. Obviously, there is a cycle to the lives of women's networks. You repeat certain activities while you move on to new ones. Recognizing and responding to change is a perfect example of that process.

Internal Challenges

In Chapter Six, we discussed how to deal with many of the common issues that arise in a network's life span. So what makes those issues different from these? It's a question of intensity. If participation in activities has slowed for two or three months, it usually means members are busy and the slump will probably pass. If this slow period has lasted six or eight months, you may need to take stronger action. In addition, network leaders can often sense a real change in the membership. There may be rumblings of boredom or discontent or frustration that are easily felt in meetings or activities. It may be tough to target exactly what the problem is at first, but it is usually clear that something significant about the network needs to change.

The internal changes networks face can be grouped into two areas: membership needs and interests and network effectiveness. We will review common challenges in each of these areas and strategies to respond to these changes.

Membership Needs and Interests

A strong membership is the most important success factor for women's networks. So, not surprisingly, it's important for leaders to be aware of any problems in this area.

If you sense a major shift in member interests, you will want to gauge network goals again. The agenda-setting tools described in Chapter Three apply as well in this situation. If you've already used them once, go back to the ones that seemed most useful the first time—if you developed an effective membership survey, for example, consider using it again to test members' interests. If one-to-one interviews were especially revealing, go back to that strategy. Many networks use brainstorming sessions to identify membership issues. Try using a combination of two or three approaches to balance the broad data from many members and the in-depth information you can get from individuals.

Common Reasons for Low Participation

One of the most common concerns we hear from mature networks is drop-off in participation by members. If it's been going on for more than six months, it's time to think about possible causes. Low participation is usually a symptom of other issues. Some of these may be caused by the network, others may be beyond the network's control. It's crucial to identify what's going on.

• *Lack of interest in events:* Over the course of a few years, most networks need to redesign their activities and events. Member interests tend to change every few years, and so should the events. Networks that recruit a number of new members at once are especially prone to this. It's necessary to check back and find out what members are interested in *now* and adjust goals and activities to reflect those interests—otherwise, the network will find itself working very hard to satisfy an audience that no longer exists. Depending on how different member interests are now, you may also need to change the mission and goals of the network as a whole.

One network had a number of well-attended networking events their first year. After ten to twelve months, however, participation started to go down. Investigating this symptom further, organizers realized that members were ready to move on to more substantive career development events. Attendance rose again when the network began scheduling those activities.

• *Lack of time to devote to the network:* This is a very common problem. To respond to it, you don't need to reexamine the overall goals of the network. Instead, you need to streamline them. However, you need to understand exactly what members are looking for before you start cutting activities. Once you've done some data gathering and have a clear sense of member interests, start eliminating the activities that don't directly respond to those needs. Also think about cutting any activities that take a great deal of time and energy to coordinate. Keep in mind that ten networking events use half the planning needed for one conference. So reduce time stress by thinking about what members are interested in and what kinds of events require the least work on their part—and yours.

Obsolete Membership Criteria

The other significant membership transition networks often face is changing the membership itself. Any network with membership criteria that limit participation in any way will at some point face the decision of whether to expand. Most networks decide to expand after two to five years of existence. Managing this transition is critical to ensuring the long-term health of the network. Doing it well can also revitalize a network and give it a wider range of options.

> We did, after the first year and a half, expand from that higher-level group of women, so it's open to everybody. We've gotten new blood and a new infusion of energy, and it also took away some of that criticism that we didn't deal with for the first year or so.
>
> *—Women's network leader*

It's especially important to be flexible as you expand your membership. New members will have different agendas and goals, and the network needs to incorporate them into the mission and activities. Here are some suggestions for making this transition as smooth as possible:

• *Reconfigure your leadership team to reflect your entire membership.* If new members are going to join, they need to see representatives of their level, function, or location represented in your steering group.

• *Have the leadership team conduct an internal climate survey for the newly created membership.* You want to understand the interests of new members, but also take time to poll the longstanding members. Take the time to examine the membership as a whole and create new goals and activities. That way you won't create a hierarchy of needs with old members first and new members second—or vice versa.

• *Be sensitive in your outreach.* As you solicit new members, consider your approach. Many times, the outreach of a network that originally involved senior women or was based only at headquarters has been perceived as paternalistic or heavy-handed. Approach new members as equals and stress that point in all verbal and written communications. Most companies have natural tensions among levels and between corporate and field locations. Be careful to avoid adding to the stress along predictable organizational fault lines.

> We have some very clear challenges ahead of us. We have dividing lines between women who are in management or the professional ranks versus the staff/secretarial functions. We also have a clear dividing line between the scientist type and the nonscientist type. And then we have the senior-level management against everybody else.
>
> —*Women's network leader*

• *Communicate the network's change in membership and goals to the organization.* As with all major changes in the network, transitions in membership should be highlighted to your constituencies. In some cases, networks relaunch themselves with a new name and approach. Create a special edition of your newsletter or plan an event to communicate this change in the network to everyone who needs to know.

Networks that have expanded their membership recognize that it's often a bumpy road. There are new interests, goals, underlying agendas, and audiences. It often takes a full six months to a year to make this transition. So don't be concerned if it doesn't happen overnight. It's one of the largest steps a network can take, and one that should be guided carefully.

Network Effectiveness

Sometimes, the network runs smoothly and accomplishes a great deal. Other times, even a simple decision or event can take far too much time and energy. As with the membership changes, consider the intensity of the problem before deciding to take drastic action.

When Goals Seem Out of Reach

Sometimes, a network has an inability to reach goals or accomplish activities. Again, this tends to be a symptom rather than the problem itself.

One Network Redefines Itself—Bausch & Lomb

At the end of 1995, Bausch & Lomb's Women's Executive Network, which had been for executive women only, considered expanding its membership to include more women and created a steering committee of interested women from different levels and divisions in the company's Rochester facility. The network hired an outside consulting firm to conduct an e-mail survey of female employees and gauge the interest in creating a network for all of them. The result? Strong support for the network, with particular interest in career and leadership issues, work/life balance, and networking with other women (just two or three among almost two hundred returned surveys indicated negative response). In 1996, the Women's Network at Bausch & Lomb opened its membership to all B&L employees, both male and female.

Network leadership had feared they would be too busy to manage an enlarged network, but it turned out that they functioned as mentors as other women stepped in to leadership roles. The network held its kickoff event in 1996, with B&L's chairman, CEO, and HR VP all in attendance. One-third to one-half of all female salaried employees at the Rochester site were there, too, including a good core group of women to organize future events.

Expanding the network erased the negativity that had resulted from hourly workers perceiving that executive women didn't see them as "important" enough to include. The inclusion of men, either as members or welcome participants in events, helps eliminate the perception that women are receiving "special treatment."

The network now organizes special interest groups within the larger group. They can be organized by level, function, or issues of special interest such as professional growth or mentoring. For more on the Bausch & Lomb women's network, see Resource B.

Sometimes the cause of the problem comes from factors inside the network. If the leadership is out of touch with the members and the membership doesn't support the overall goals and mission of the network, nothing will go right for it. You'll see a similar pattern if the activities are out of tune with goals and mission the members do support—if they're not interested, they won't show up.

Alternatively, the weakness may be in the leadership structure itself. If there are too many or too few leaders to prioritize and guide the network's goals and activities, it will waste its energies. Leaders may also be too concerned about making the early activities "perfect"—and fall into a paralysis of overplanning that prevents them from taking any action. The leadership group may simply lack the time to lead and roll out the events they've scheduled—either because they're overburdened with other responsibilities or because they've scheduled too many activities, which results in too little attention devoted to each goal or event.

But even a network with a good grasp of its mission, an interested and active membership, and solid leadership can run into trouble. If external stakeholders—senior management, Human Resources, anyone with whom the network must partner to achieve goals or conduct activities—decide to withhold support, it's much more difficult to proceed. Likewise, sweat equity is not enough—the network needs to develop sufficient physical resources in terms of funding and access to facilities for the activities its members need.

Once you've identified the driver of the problem, consider solutions carefully. If the issue is membership, return to Chapter Two and Chapter Five to design strategies to solicit and respond to member needs. If the problem is a lack of senior-level support, consult Chapter Four to create an approach to build and maintain support.

When There's Nothing Left to Do

On the other side of the spectrum, some networks face a situation where they have fulfilled their goals with no clear next steps.

> We have too much of a good thing. The efforts of the group are totally institutionalized in the corporate culture. That's why we can't focus on goals. Everything is already in place.
>
> —*Women's network leader*

It's an ironically difficult place to find yourself in. You've accomplished your goals and fulfilled your mission. Now what? Here are some options: You can regroup and come up with other goals. The network can focus more on informal social activities and less on the advisory role. It can expand its efforts into the community or to other companies. It can also wind up its affairs. (See later in this chapter for strategies to conclude a network.)

Let the membership decide. Networks in this situation often find that an open membership meeting is the place to make that decision. Surveys or interviews do not work well, because it is a groupwide and often emotional decision. Take time to congratulate yourselves on reaching an enviable point and then figure out what the next steps are.

When No One Takes the Reins

Finally, a significant transition can occur during times when there are no leaders. Sometimes, there simply is no one who can lead the network. The current leader may be moving to a new position within the company or leaving the company altogether. No one is able to take on that leadership role, either by choice or necessity. So, a decision needs to be made. How can the network continue to function without a clear leader?

You can continue, but it often requires a significant scaling down of activities. Since it is so difficult to create a large event without leadership, groups often focus on informal networking activities. Events such as speakers series or conferences are usually not possible. Sometimes networks continue on indefinitely at this stage, with low-intensity events and no formal leadership. Other times, a leader will become apparent and take on that role. In those cases, the network often restarts itself.

One final note about leadership. A lack of leadership is often a function of time availability and who has it. However, it can be a red flag for an off-course network. If members have time to devote to leadership roles but choose not to do so, that may mean the network isn't focused on their needs. Before you assume the lack of leaders is a question of time commitments, make sure it doesn't reflect a larger problem of differing missions and goals among members and the network.

External Challenges

The other type of significant change facing networks comes from the outside. While many of the day-to-day decisions facing network leaders relate to the internal workings of the network, some of the most significant changes are caused by companywide events.

Economic Downturns

In today's economic climate, many networks exist in companies where there are workforce reductions or major organizational shifts. When this happens, networks need to ask themselves a few questions:

• *How will this affect network members?* During any time of transition in an organization, everybody does more work. For the women's network, this often means that members have less time to devote to network activities. It also can change members' priorities and interests. Smart networks recognize that this type of environment requires a change in focus and activities.

Things are flattening out and it's difficult for people to advance. One of the things that we face continually is the dispirited women who just feel like there's nothing to do and no place to go. How do you enrich their work experience or how do you enrich their lives? We're trying to focus more on interesting roles

and more on some work/life balance stuff. Members need to go get some good-
ies someplace besides their job because it just isn't enough anymore.

—Women's network leader

Many networks scale back their activities during such a phase. However, it's
important to be very careful about the events you eliminate. Some networks eliminate networking and focus on career development workshops because members
are more conscious of the need to have marketable skills in an uncertain work environment. Other networks slow down career development activities and redou-
ble their networking events. This strategy responds to members who either want
support from colleagues or want to network as a way to develop contacts in other
areas. Few networks stop their activities altogether—after all, members still benefit from the group. However, there is a refocusing on member needs and direct
services the network can provide.

• *How will this affect the network's role within the organization?* During major organizational shifts or cutbacks, anything that isn't core to the business is questioned.
So it becomes that much more important for the network to prove its worth. You've
spent a great deal of time building support for the group, and it's particularly important to maintain this support during a time of economic uncertainty. In considering the events you create, think about two things—*level of visibility* and *broad
appeal.*

Depending on what type of event you sponsor, visibility during a company
transition can be both good and bad. Given the focus on dollars and how they're
spent, you want to pay close attention to anything that might appear to be lavish
or a waste of money. For example, many networks stop having annual conferences
at times like these. They're often big and well-publicized, and can stir up resentment from other parts of the company. Think about the expensive events you run
and consider ways to scale them back. If you can meet those same goals with low-
key events requiring less money, all the better.

Smart networks also reach out to a broader audience during these times. Helping members is important, but the more you help employees in general, the more
support you'll build and the more impact you'll have. Many networks focus on
broad career development workshops that are open to large numbers of employees.

During several downsizing efforts we've run résumé writing workshops. Some
people had never written a résumé before. So we ran résumé writing workshops
and interviewing workshops because they were going within the corporation for
interviews.

—Women's network leader

As a corporation we are going through—pick the word—reengineering, restructuring, downsizing, rightsizing. The service we offer is any member who is
put on the bubble could send their résumé in to the steering committee and we
would do our best to help them out, or get their résumé to somebody else.

—Women's network leader

When layoffs were happening, we started support groups for the people who
were being laid off and the people who weren't. They worked together and followed up leads to find out about conferences and job fairs and help with résumé writing.

—Women's network leader

• *How will this affect the network leadership?* Corporate restructuring affects both
members and leaders. If the network leaders are high-level, they may be asked to
relocate to a new headquarters location, they may be involved with company strategy teams, or they may leave the organization. Whatever the reason, a network
facing a vacuum in leadership needs to take action.

If you've built a strong succession plan, then you should have a leader in place
relatively quickly. However, many members have more work and are less likely
to volunteer for leadership positions. In this situation, networks often shrink their
activity base and focus on fewer and smaller goals that require less formal leadership.

We've gone through a couple of reorganizations and layoffs. Our core team
had eight people and six were laid off or relocated. So we got to the point
where there were three or four of us holdovers trying to keep the group together. We were at a crossroads. We could just be an organization where we
could get together on a monthly basis and chit-chat. Or we could try to resur-
rect our goals and move forward. Our new charter is very scaled back. We
don't sponsor events on a regular monthly basis anymore, but we try to do
something at least every other month and we decide as a team what issues are
important that year.

—Women's network leader

Changes in Senior Leadership

The other significant external issue for networks is a change in relationship with
a senior champion. Sometimes an executive sponsor leaves the organization, or
moves to a new role. Either way, that individual can no longer support the network in the same way and the network loses that sponsorship. Other times (and

this is especially true during downsizing) an entire executive team can leave. This can be difficult for network leaders because they need to both establish new executive champions and build support among a new senior team.

Whatever the situation you find yourself in, you should return to your original strategies to build support. Look back at the activities described in Chapter Four to gain credibility and support from senior management and apply them to the new team. First, though, you need to do a reality check. If your champion has left but there are other supportive people still on the management team, then it's an issue of cultivating and working with a new senior team member. If, however, you need to rebuild support from the beginning, recognize that this will require a different set of strategies. You'll need to move more slowly and put in more time and effort to reach this individual or senior group.

In addition, there is often a ripple effect on the network as a whole. Depending on how deep the network's roots are in the organization, you may or may not need to scale back your activities. A relatively new network that was just getting ready to present recommendations to senior management will need to drop back and build more support first. On the other hand, a more established network may be able to go straight on without reducing its activity level. Instead, its leadership probably needs to spend more time building support among management and educating them about its activities and impact. Whatever the situation is, be realistic about your opportunities and the work you'll need to do to build back those relationships.

Ending the Network

For some networks, internal or external pressures are significant enough to raise the question of disbanding the group. If that is the decision you make, it's absolutely critical to control the process. The key is to make an informed decision to end the network, understand the implications of the decision, and communicate that decision to the company. It's sometimes difficult to know if you're at that point and how to do it. Here are some signposts to watch for along the way:

Common Reasons for Disbanding a Network

- It has fulfilled its mission; its activities are integrated into the organizational systems.
- Its membership is no longer interested in participating in network due to time constraints or personal needs and interests, and women not already in the network do not join it.
- Its company decides to prohibit formal employee networks.

Litigation: Why and How to Manage the Network's Interest

These days, there are more and more suits over sexual harassment or gender discrimination being filed. Especially if a case gains publicity, a network can be in a delicate situation. On one hand, networks want to be supportive to the individuals filing suit, especially if they are members. On the other hand, supporting an individual who is suing the company can erode or destroy the network's support among management. It's impossible to know all the details of a case—and involving the network in a lawsuit in any way can lead to legal ramifications for the group itself. For these reasons, Catalyst recommends that in most cases networks remain neutral as organizations.

Individual members may then choose to support or assist the plaintiff, but they should make absolutely clear they are acting as individuals, not as representatives of the network. You don't know all the facts and any involvement can create more problems. It's almost always best for the network per se to be uninvolved in lawsuits, and to state as clearly as necessary that the network is not part of any proceedings.

- Its leadership cannot maintain the role and no members are interested in taking on leadership positions.

You'll notice that some of the reasons listed here are also highlighted in the membership section of this chapter. And some of the same issues are also highlighted in Chapter Six. As network leaders, you can tell the difference between a situation that can be addressed through modifications and a more intense, serious problem. It's best to address these issues head-on, and that involves discussing them with the entire membership.

Such a discussion will also ensure that you're not making assumptions about member goals. For example, you may not be able to continue as a leader and you think there's no one to fill the position. Without bringing it up in front of the membership, you'll never know for sure. Someone may surprise you and offer to take over. It's equally likely that someone may not. However, you will have at least solicited the full membership and made an informed decision.

Questions to Ask Before Disbanding

We can't stress enough how important it is to bring the full membership into these discussions. This is one of the most important decisions the network will make and you want to make it as a group. This also will give you the opportunity to discuss the ramifications of ending the network and determine the necessary follow-up work. The following questions will help you consider the matter in an orderly fashion:

• *What services and activities does the network provide?* Consider what career or networking resources the network offers to members and other employees. Are there other departments within the company or outside organizations that also provide those services? If they do exist in other parts of the organization, communicate that to your various audiences.

• *Do members want to continue to meet informally?* This often happens after the dissolution of the formal network. Members still get together for lunches or after work to socialize. Encourage that to happen if there's an interest, but recognize that it's completely informal. If it looks like people want it to be more formal, then you may have a different type of network in the works. Informal get-togethers are still a network, and you can recreate your network to accomplish that goal.

• *How will you communicate the network's ending to the company?* There is nothing more disheartening than a network that ends bit by bit and never formally communicates its resolution. Everyone in the company who knows about the network's creation should also know when it ends. As with all communications strategies, you should create formal and informal vehicles. Most networks create a notice or newsletter outlining the fact that the network is ending, the reasons why, and the other resources available for interested parties. You should also communicate directly with targeted individuals in senior management, Human Resources, other employee networks, and other involved groups. Meeting personally with these stakeholders ensures that your message is sent clearly and that they understand why the network is ending.

One final note. At many companies, networks existed years ago that few people know about now. One or two individuals may remember that there once was

---

Yes, There Are Happy Endings, Too

Avon Products is a case in point. A women's network existed briefly at Avon, but its goals were met in large part by management. Could that be because women make up 80 percent of Avon's management? Certainly it could, and is. Avon is also the home of several other successful and inclusive employee networks, including a Black Professional Association, Asian and Hispanic employee networks, and a parents' network. Employees pursue various non-gender-linked goals through those entities.

a network, but they know little about its purpose, mission, and goals. Whatever good it did is largely lost to the company. When your network closes down, however, it doesn't need to join the ranks of forgotten experiments.

Bear in mind that it's very likely that another women's network will form sometime in the future in your company. To ensure that its organizers know about your network and can learn from your experience, be sure to document the creation and activities of the network. Highlight why it was formed, what the goals were, what you accomplished, and why you decided to disband. Include a list of the leadership so that future networks can contact them, if they still work at the company. Place copies of this information in various parts of the organization, such as in Human Resources or the executive offices. In this way, you're ensuring the network will continue to have an influence in some form even after its end.

Checklist

☐ Identify major shifts, internal or external, facing the network.

☐ Conduct a thorough analysis of the situation to determine the primary causes.

☐ Involve the membership in evaluating and responding to the situation.

☐ Design and implement an appropriate response that integrates the network's ability to change and member goals and interests.

☐ Clearly communicate any major changes in the network to audiences within the company.

☐ Include the membership in any decision to end the network.

☐ Communicate the dissolution of the network to the organization.

☐ Leave a clear and readily accessible record of what the network did.

CEO SUPPORT FROM THE BEGINNING: KODAK

Origins. Kodak women had been meeting at informal dinners for a few years. Finally, the CEO appeared at one such event and challenged the group to become a formal network and to engage managers throughout the organization. That CEO support made it all happen.

Support. Because of the CEO's constant and visible backing, large numbers of managers became involved in the network. The Kodak Diversity Office was also very helpful—it acts as a link between all the company's networks and key managers. At Kodak, all managers need to engage in at least three or four diversity-related activities every year; network events count toward that total. The network has also put together a Briefing Book, modeled on the way Kodak communicates initiatives, which is distributed to any manager or leader who is interested in the network. (See Resource B-3 for some sample material from this book.) It includes background on the network—including a multi-page chart that sets out "barriers that women face in the workplace" and offers strategies for employees, managers, and networks to help overcome them—plus copies of network newsletters, recent speeches by network leaders, and the results of network surveys, as well as the network's vision and mission. Last year, a total of two hundred briefing books were distributed.

Vision. The Women's Forum vision encompasses working with management "for the betterment of Kodak as a preferred employer in Rochester and worldwide." Elements included in that vision are career development, communication, diversity, environment, equality, leadership, mentoring, and networking.

Membership. The Women's Forum is open to all Kodak employees—men, too, belong to the women's network. It all started at that first dinner that the CEO attended. Someone invited him to join and he accepted. Then a few key senior leaders became members to show their support. And finally male employees began asking how they could join. They had noticed that some of the network's events could benefit men as well as women—career development seminars, for instance. So now the network invites men to events and solicits them for membership just as they always have with women. And many men attend, and find many ways to benefit. For a recent educational event on breast cancer awareness and mammography, for example, men brought their wives and daughters.

Major Activities. Leaders, managers, and all employees turn out in force for the network's highly visible annual dinner, which is interactive and business-focused rather than gender-based. They aren't "just social get-togethers, which no one has time for." Those dinners have also been instrumental in building support from management. When managers who attend talk to their colleagues about the event, the colleagues often join them the following year. In 1998, close to three hundred people attended the Spring Managers' Forum, about 40 percent of them managers. The remaining 60 percent of attendees were network members, a third of them men.

The forum's other ongoing activity is arranging monthly Manager Get-Togethers. These are regularly scheduled events that bring employees and a manager together for small-group discussions on issues that affect everyone at Kodak. Topics include diversity, career development, business goals, opportunities at Kodak, and the "enablers and inhibitors" of women's success at Kodak. Member surveys show that manager get-togethers are among the most valuable events put on by the network, with nonmembers and members attending in equal numbers. The managers also give them high marks—one leader even uses them to identify potential talent among employees. He looks for participants who ask good questions and participate skillfully, then thinks about them when there are openings in his organization.

Advisory Role. Women's Forum members have found that their extensive informal interaction with management is a highly effective way to fulfill a network's advisory capacity.

EPILOGUE

SUMMING UP: WOMEN'S NETWORKS MEAN BUSINESS

In its thirty-some years of working with business to advance women, Catalyst has learned a great deal about how women and networks work. In all that time, we have discovered only positive things about women's networks. There is no downside to employees' coming together to help each other and their organization get ahead. Women's networks can be seen (and are seen, by more and more companies lucky enough to be run by enlightened management) simply as one more tool—a highly effective, fresh, and innovative tool—for improving the bottom line.

Creating Women's Networks is not a book to read once and then go on to the next page-turner. It's a step-by-step guide to setting up and running the sort of network that builds strength for its members and for the company they work in. The deeper you dig into its pages, the more you'll get out of it.

In conclusion, Catalyst wishes you well with your brand-new (or revitalized) network. If creating a network seems like a great deal of work, keep in mind how significant its success will be for you, your colleagues, and your company—and that each step is relatively simple. Whatever the time you have available, you can make a go of it if you choose goals and activities tailored to your needs and environment—and find enough like-minded people to help. One thing we're sure of: both you and your company will be the better for having a full-fledged women's network as part of your lives.

CATALYST'S SUMMARY FINDINGS FROM THE WOMEN'S WORKPLACE NETWORK SURVEY

Catalyst's survey on women's workplace networks consisted of two parts. Part A was designed for a management representative familiar with the women's network, if one existed. Part B was to be filled out by the leader of the women's network at the company.

Respondents

A total of 132 companies participated in our survey on women's workplace networks. The following is a breakdown of responding companies by industry, revenues, and number of employees.

Industry	Respondent (percent)
Services	45
Manufacturing: Durable	33
Manufacturing: Nondurable	22

Revenues	Respondent (percent)
<$1 billion	16
$1 billion—$5 billion	36
$5 billion—$100 billion	45
>$100 billion	3

Number of employees	Respondent (percent)
<1,000	5
1,000–5,000	18
5,000–20,000	32
20,000–50,000	34
>50,000	11

About the Companies

To gain background information on responding companies and programs they offered, Part A of the survey included questions on the existence of various employee networks and on the existence of programs or initiatives related to flexible work options, career development, and diversity. From these responses, Catalyst researchers were able to determine the prevalence of these networks and initiatives, as well as to explore linkages among them.

Employee Networks

The most common networks in companies are women's groups. Overall, 34 percent of responding companies have a women's network. Almost equally represented are African American networks, noted by 33 percent of companies. Just under 20 percent of companies have Asian American networks, Latino networks, or gay and lesbian networks.

Network type	Respondent (percent)
Women	34
African American	33
Asian American	17
Latino	19
Gay and Lesbian	17

Women's Networks

Those companies that have women's networks are much more likely to have other employee networks.

Other network	Companies with a women's network (percent)	Companies without a women's network (percent)
African American	62	18
Asian American	33	8
Latino	42	6
Gay and Lesbian	40	5

Twenty percent of management representatives at companies without a women's network were considering creating one in the future. This percentage may or may not reflect the opinion of women in the company, who may be considering the formation of a women's network. Fourteen percent of these companies had had a women's network in the past.

About the Women's Networks

The first set of questions for companies with women's networks were general, and related to overall characteristics and size. We found that groups had an average of 159 members, and a median of 100 members. Almost 50 percent of groups were created between 1992 and 1994. The median length of existence for groups was four years.

Companies with Women's Networks

We were also interested in the types of companies that had women's workplace networks. On average, those companies with women's networks were larger; the average number of employees at such a company was 19,300. The distribution of companies by industry was relatively even, reflecting an overrepresentation of nondurable manufacturing companies as compared with the overall sample.

Number of employees	Companies with women's networks
1,000–5,000	3
5,000–20,000	48
20,000–50,000	35
>50,000 Employees	14

Industry	Companies with women's networks
Services	38
Manufacturing: Nondurable	33
Manufacturing: Durable	29

Frequency and Level of Women's Networks

Part A of the survey asked how many women's groups existed at the organization, and at what level. The majority of responding companies with women's networks reported having more than one group within the organization. The most common level for a women's group was the corporate level. Many also exist at the divisional level or at a plant or field location, indicating an increased specialization of focus for these groups.

Level of group	Respondent (percent)
Corporate	84
Division	44
Plant or field location	29
Regional	20

Who Initiated Women's Network?

Women's workplace networks can be created by individuals at any level within an organization. In this survey, respondents indicated there was often more than one initiator of the group, pointing to women's groups being created as a result of overlapping needs by a number of groups, including women at various levels, Human Resources, and management.

Initiator	Respondent (percent)
Senior women	49
Mid-level women	49
Entry-level women	12
Human Resources	10
Senior-level management	8
Nonexempt women	6
CEO	6

Who Are the Members

An issue facing all women's networks is membership. Groups struggle with what levels to include, as well as whether to include men as well as women. Among survey respondents, the majority of groups (63 percent) are made up of women only. Of that group, almost 40 percent are for professional-level women only. Twenty-five percent of the groups were open to both men and women, at all levels within the organization.

Resources Provided by the Company and Women's Network

Two questions were asked to gain insight into the resources or services the women's network and company provide to one another. The most common resource given to the women's network is facilities for meetings. Additionally, over half of companies provide a budget to the group, and just under half provide a liaison to the group, usually from Human Resources. Less than one quarter of all groups charge fees to their members.

Resource provided by company	Respondent (percent)
Company facilities	88
Budget	51
Company liaison	45
Information from Human Resources	43

Almost half of the women's networks act in an advisory role to the company. Of those that do, the overwhelming majority advise both Human Resources and senior management.

Resource provided by women's network	Respondent (percent)
Advise senior management	47
Advise Human Resources	47
Participate in diversity efforts	19

Relationships Among Employee Networks

The majority of women's groups surveyed interact with other employee networks (61 percent). Almost 20 percent also interact with other women's networks in their company. Over half work with the diversity council in their organization.

Why Was a Women's Network Formed?

The survey found a wide range of reasons for forming a women's network. The most common reasons cited were the desire for networking among women and the need to educate the company on women's issues. Note: Percentages in the following table don't add up to 100 because respondents could indicate multiple reasons.

Impetus for starting women's network	Agreement (percent)
Networking for women	51
Educate company and management on women's issues	45
Develop opportunities for women	35
Create a better workplace for women	31
Women in company interested in forming network	25
Lack of women in management positions	16

What Are the Most Important Issues for the Women's Network?

The top issues for these groups are networking and career development and advancement, reflecting the important roles networks play in helping women advance in their careers and enhance their job-related skills.

Area of importance	"Of Critical Importance" or "Very Important" (percent)
Networking	90
Career development and advancement	88
Diversity issues	82
Mentoring programs	77
Work and family issues	76
Sexual harassment issues	55
Implementing flexible work arrangements	35

Activities of the Women's Network

The top five activities reported in the survey further reinforce the networking and career development-related missions of women's networks. More than three-quarters of groups sponsor speakers, 71 percent have networking events, and more than 50 percent of groups have mentoring programs or other career development activities.

Activity	Respondent (percent)
Speakers	83
Networking events	71
Seminars and workshops	67
Career development events	65
Mentoring programs	55

Groups Served by the Women's Network

Women's networks have clear groups within the organization they target, as reflected in their mission statements as well as their membership criteria. Both women's networks and management clearly see professional-level women as the primary population served by a women's network. Interestingly, management liaisons see both senior management and senior-level women as being of greater importance than the women's networks do.

Additionally, while both groups rank employees not in the women's network as last in importance, the women's networks see the importance of this group as significantly higher than the management liaisons did. Overall, however, the sets of responses were quite similar.

	"Of Critical Importance" or "Very Important" (percent)	
Populations served	Women's network	Management
Professional level women	76	71
Human Resources	54	51
Senior management	53	60
Nonexempt women	43	38
Senior-level women	41	51
Middle management	37	31
Employees not in women's network	22	9

Roles Women's Networks Play

To build on the survey data regarding networks' purpose and mission, Catalyst asked an open-ended question about the roles of the women's networks. This question was posed to leaders of the group as well as to management.

Overall, the areas defined by both sets of respondents were quite similar. In fact, the top four areas were the same for both groups, *and in the same order*. The networking/support role was the top response. Management, however, viewed this role as much more significant than the women's network leaders did. In general, the women's network leaders' responses were more evenly distributed among the top four categories, while the management responses targeted certain roles more clearly.

It is important to note that almost three-quarters of management respondents saw the women's network taking on an advisory role to management. Additionally, 11 percent of management respondents saw one network role as providing management with names of high-potential women for developmental or advancement opportunities.

	Respondent (percent)	
Role of women's network	Women's network (percent)	Management (percent)
Networking/support	57	96
Adviser to management	51	69
Career development	45	58
Vehicle for organizational change	37	49

Positive Responses to Women's Network

When asked to comment on the types and range of positive responses the women's group has received within the organization, almost all respondents indicated there had been either significant or some positive response. Women's network leaders indicated a greater percentage of significant positive responses, while management placed the majority of positive response in the "some positive response" category.

	Management (percent)	Women's network leaders (percent)
Significant positive response	36	49
Some positive response	53	41
Minor positive response	4	4
Don't know	7	4
Did not answer	0	2

When asked to outline the specific types of positive responses to the women's network, 60 percent of management respondents noted that senior management uses the women's network. Fifty-six percent of management respondents indicated that the group was seen as a positive force within the company. Thirty-one percent indicated that women's issues are better understood within the company because of the work of the women's network, and 11 percent pointed to the leadership experience gained by members of the women's group. Other examples cited by management include the group networking with the diversity council, the external recognition of the group and its leaders, and the increased involvement of males in the group's activities.

The women's network leaders cited fewer specific examples of positive responses. Fifty percent indicated that senior management uses the group, and 39 percent mentioned that women's issues are better understood within the company because of the group's efforts.

Negative Responses to Women's Network

Catalyst also wanted to learn about any negative responses women's networks were experiencing. Again, this question was asked of both the women's network leaders and of management. It is clear that very few groups experience significant backlash, and 20 percent of groups experience no backlash whatsoever.

Almost 75 percent of responses from management and women's networks indicate, though, that groups are experiencing some form of backlash, although it may be minor. Network leaders feel that their groups experience more backlash than management representatives seem to see, as indicated by the higher percentage of women's network leaders' responses in the "Significant" and "Some negative response" categories. That difference of about 15 percent appears to be distributed by the management to the "Minor" category.

	Management (percent)	Women's network leaders (percent)
Significant negative response	0	4
Some negative response	20	31
Minor negative response	53	39
No negative response	18	20
Don't know	9	2
Did not answer	0	4

When asked to give examples of negative reactions to the women's network, almost 50 percent of network leaders pointed to males being threatened by the group's existence. Other examples included criticism related to the elitism of the group, criticism directed to group leaders or members anonymously, concern by women about how their participation in the women's network would affect their career or position within the company, and conflicts between the group's role and the role of Human Resources.

Responses from management highlighted a lack of knowledge about the group (29 percent) and males being threatened by the group's existence (22 percent). Management respondents also pointed to elitism or lack of diversity within the group, concerns about the group's effectiveness, and lack of management support for the network.

DOW CHEMICAL WIN CHANGE PROCESS

A diagram like that on the next page is very effective in clarifying the purpose of a network. It serves as the Dow Women's Innovation Network's mission statement.

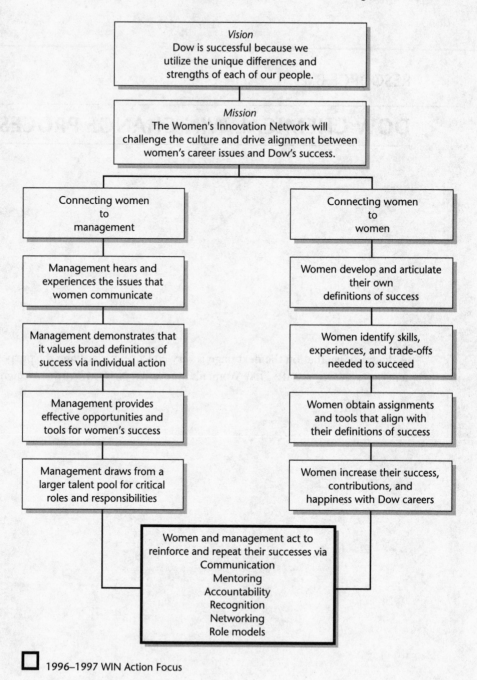

Vision
Dow is successful because we
utilize the unique differences and
strengths of each of our people.

Mission
The Women's Innovation Network will
challenge the culture and drive alignment between
women's career issues and Dow's success.

Connecting women
to
management

Connecting women
to
women

Management hears and
experiences the issues that
women communicate

Women develop and articulate
their own
definitions of success

Management demonstrates that
it values broad definitions of
success via individual action

Women identify skills,
experiences, and trade-offs
needed to succeed

Management provides
effective opportunities and
tools for women's success

Women obtain assignments
and tools that align with
their definitions of success

Management draws from a
larger talent pool for critical
roles and responsibilities

Women increase their success,
contributions, and
happiness with Dow careers

Women and management act to
reinforce and repeat their successes via
Communication
Mentoring
Accountability
Recognition
Networking
Role models

1996–1997 WIN Action Focus

BAUSCH & LOMB'S DIVERSITY CHECKLIST

This list was created by the Bausch & Lomb women's network to give executives concrete examples of actions they could take immediately to improve women's opportunities at the company.

☐ When a developmental opportunity arises (an internal task force, an executive education course, a cross-functional rotation), I make sure that women are considered.

☐ I participate in a regular review process to ensure that women are progressing satisfactorily against established measures of progress.

☐ I personally serve as a mentor to at least one female manager, and each of my direct reports does the same.

☐ I host at least two business-related social events per year in which management women can participate comfortably.

☐ I support women employees' networks and meet regularly with their representatives to discuss gender-based issues in the company.

☐ I send clear and frequent messages to my team that fostering diversity in management is important to the productivity and competitiveness of the company and that I am personally committed to it.

☐ I actively intervene in meetings or conversations in which interrupting, stifling, or other behavior infringes on the full participation of women participants.

☐ I respect the fact that the majority of my employees are part of dual-earner or single-parent families and make it possible for them to balance work and personal responsibilities by supporting use of policies such as flexible work and parental leave.

☐ I provide occasions for female directors of my company to meet with executive and management women.

☐ I serve as a director, volunteer, or member of at least one organization in which I am in the minority by gender or race.

☐ I have a system for identifying and developing high-potential managers and ensure fair representation of women in that pool.

☐ Women in my company are well represented in line management positions and in functions from which senior managers are typically drawn.

KODAK EMPLOYEES BRIEFING BOOK: SELECTED ITEMS FROM A NETWORK GUIDE

The Women's Forum of Kodak Employees provides a useful model for network development in a large organization. This section presents some of the materials the forum uses to define itself and its programs.

Mission

The Women's Forum is an organization open to all Kodak employees to promote excellence and facilitate diversity by providing development opportunities for women through mentoring, networking, and training so that there is a positive environment for growth and advancement at Eastman Kodak. The Women's Forum leaders and members will demonstrate support of the five Kodak values in all our actions and communications.

Vision

Kodak management and the Women's Forum partner together for the betterment of Kodak as a preferred employer in the Rochester community and worldwide. This vision encompasses eight guiding principles and applies to women at all levels.

Eight Guiding Principles

- *Career Development:* Women have the same career development opportunities as men.
- *Communication:* There is a productive interaction between management and individual network members.
- *Diversity:* Every employee's potential is maximized independent of gender.
- *Environment:* The corporate environment fosters career growth and mutual respect. People and their ideas are valued.
- *Equality:* Women are fully recognized and valued for their capabilities and contributions to the company.
- *Leadership:* Kodak women hold leadership and management positions at all levels and lead key projects.
- *Mentoring:* Mentors and coaches (peer and senior, male and female) occur naturally for women.
- *Networking:* A flexible framework exists for women to informally share information, experiences, and mutual concerns.

Organizational Structure

Women's Forum of Kodak Employees Board of Directors

Six Elected Board Members Executive Officers	Executive Officers President President Elect Secretary Treasurer Parliamentarian
• Develop long-range strategic goals for WFKE • Identify issues salient to WFKE members • Act as resource to those seeking information on working women's issues • Approve the annual operating budget • Approve Affiliate Chapters	• Provide day-to-day management of WFKE • Organize all WFKE business activities including general business meetings • Implement the programs and strategies of the organization • Establish the annual dues • Chair the organization's standing committees

1998 Initiatives

1. Successful Mentoring, Leadership, and Career Development

Leader:

Deniz Schildkraut/Connie Kaminski—Career Development

Sue Burke/Cyd Dunne/Connie Kaminski—Mentoring

Laura Brooks/Cyd Dunne—Board Mentoring

Sue Burke/Leslie Henckler/Darcey Johnson—Leadership

Goals:

- Continue with Manager Get-Togethers
- Survey membership for follow-up on people's activities
- Schedule one Career Development Event
- Schedule one Leadership Development Event
- Identify Salary Schedule 1 Leadership Development Training Opportunities
- Update Board on Mentoring Development Process
- Coordinate Mary Jo Spears Award

Status:

- Mentoring initiative was begun at Manager's Forum
- Ongoing Manager Get-Togethers
- Providing Leadership Development Opportunity to the Board
- Passed audit for continuing as a nonprofit organization
- Identified leadership courses for Salary Schedule 1 women

2. Lead Corporate Healing, Respect, Honor and Value Women

Leader:

Deb Brennan, Alice Valentin, Cyd Dunne

Goals:

- Follow up with National Women's Hall of Fame for nominees
- Model respect, honor, and value women in our everyday work activities and behaviors
- Coordinate speaker for Annual Dinner on this topic
- Publicize Kodak Grant

Status:

- Contacted and built relationship with Corporate Diversity and Work/Life leaders
- Provided Challenges of Change workshop for those impacted by downsizing
- Determined and communicated 150th Anniversary celebrations and events
- Publicized Kodak's traveling exhibit for 150th Anniversary celebration
- Presented Jane Lanphear Award to Karen Smith Pilkington

3. Successful Marketing Strategy for a Positive Image of WFKE

Leader:

Robin Wagstrom-Arnone—Membership

Deb Brennan—Communications

Goals:

- Develop better advertising tools
- Develop basic presentation for general presentation
- Alter demographics of membership
- Increase membership over goal (300)
- Utilize the Web for enhanced communications

Status:

- Met goal of 300 members
- Acquired demographic information

4. Participate in Corporate Connections

Leader:

Rosita Schieble

Goals:

- Share best practices
- Help networks get started
- Help members of other networks get started
- Keep WFKE members informed of what's going on in the world and other networks

Status:

- A meeting was held June 8th for Board members only

KIMBERLY-CLARK EMPLOYEE NETWORK DESCRIPTIONS

The networks described here are all open to any Kimberly-Clark employee who wishes to join.

NEON—New Employee Opportunity Network. The vision behind NEON is to improve the Kimberly-Clark organization by enhancing recruiting of top prospects, improving retention of employees, and increasing the initial productivity of new employees. The mission of NEON is to strengthen Kimberly-Clark by providing support, encouragement, and opportunities for personal and professional growth to new employees. This is accomplished through a series of events, activities, and individual guidance.

Adult Dependent Care Network. The mission of the Adult Dependent Care Network is to attract, retain, and improve the effectiveness of employees by providing information that leads to high-quality, cost-effective solutions of adult dependent care issues. The objectives of the group are to understand the issues related to adult dependent care and the needs of Kimberly-Clark employees, identify and publicize resources already available to address adult dependent care issues, develop a periodic forum and bring speakers to address the topics found to be of most interest for adult dependent care, and provide networking opportunities for people involved in adult dependent care issues.

Gay and Lesbian Network. The Gay and Lesbian Network of Kimberly-Clark employees provides support for gay and lesbian employees in the workplace, contributes to education and training on gay and lesbian issues, and recognizes the role of all employees in fulfilling the strategic goals of the corporation. The network invites participation by all employees, regardless of sexual orientation.

Euronet. The vision of Euronet is to develop and provide expertise to ensure that Kimberly-Clark has a broad understanding of European businesses and cultures such that the company can flexibly adapt and conduct core businesses in an effective, profitable, and respectful manner. The mission of Euronet is to be "liaisons in technology transfer." Objectives focus on internal and external technology transfer, mentoring of international transferees, and consulting as business needs arise. Euronet also offers expertise in a number of European languages and functional specializations.

WIN—Women's Interactive Network. WIN is open to all employees, women and men. The mission of WIN is to support Kimberly-Clark's achieving growth and profitability objectives by championing the organization's efforts to capitalize on the talents and contributions of its women employees. This is accomplished by offering programs, events, activities, and educational opportunities to help Kimberly-Clark attract, develop, and retain women employees.

Focus Asia. The Focus Asia Network contributes to Kimberly-Clark's objectives of best people and best products by promoting cultural awareness, increasing communication opportunities, and identifying and sharing issues of mutual concern. The Focus Asia Network achieves its objectives by inviting speakers within the corporation and the community to gain insights to the challenges facing Asians in the industry and by providing resources to the corporation on cultural issues as Kimberly-Clark continues its expansion into Asia.

AAEN—African American Employee Network. The African American Employee Network supplements Kimberly-Clark's efforts to attract and retain the best employees by aiding the career and personal development of African American employees, by providing mutual exchange of personal and professional experiences and cross-cultural understanding, and by being an available resource to management and the community.

LAND—Latin American Network for Diversity. The mission of LAND is to contribute to Kimberly-Clark's diversity initiatives by supplementing company efforts to attract, retain, and enhance the career and personal development of Hispanic employees and to serve as a resource in providing business input and direction on products and communication relevant to Hispanic and Latin American customers and consumers.

INDEX

A

AAEN. *See* African American Employee Network

Activity, major categories of, 85–86

Activity-focused committees, 46, 49

Adult Dependent Care Network (Kimberly-Clark), 179

Advising activities: and achievement of measurable objective, 114–115; checklist for, 115; and climate survey, 107–108; criteria for selecting activities for, 108–109; and educating management, 111; and identification of barriers, 111; level of involvement in, 114; and making the business case to take action 113–114; range of topics for, 110; reference list of, 111; success factors for, 112–115; and types of advisory activities, 109–112

African American Employee Network (AAEN), 180

Agenda, setting, 36–37, 38–42

American Business Collaboration for Quality Child Care, 44

American Stores, 6

Association of Women Brokers (Dain Rauscher), 4

Avon Products, 154

B

Bankers Trust, 6, 9–10, 53

Basic housekeeping: and elections and leadership succession, 122–123; and funding, 123–124; and membership meetings, 120–122

Bausch & Lomb, 147, 173–174

Bausch & Lomb executive diversity checklist, 173–174

Black Professional Association (Avon Products), 154

Brainstorming, informal, 19

Building an Effective Corporate Women's Group (Catalyst), 5

Burnout, 88

Business case, focus on, 23, 113–114

Business Women INC., 53

C

Career development events: and areas of career development, 93–94; and effective publicity, 96; effectiveness of, 96–97; involving senior leaders in, 97–98; and meeting members' needs, 96; reference list of, 94; types of programs for, 95–96

Career development programs, types of, 95–96

Catalyst Census of Corporate Officers and Top Earners, The (Catalyst), xi, 15

Challenges: checklist for, 155; and disbanding the network, 152–155; and external challenges, 149–152; and internal challenges, 143–146; and network effectiveness, 146–149

Climate. *See* Company climate

Cohesiveness, 126–129

Collegiality, 14

Commitment, 13

Committees, 46, 49–50

Communication, 60, 68

Communications strategies: and background on network, 51–52; and celebration of successes, 52; and development of feedback mechanism, 52; and importance of name, 52–53

Community, wider: and effective publicity, 106; and effectiveness, 106; and involving senior leaders, 106; and meeting members' needs, 105–106; reaching out to, 105–106

Company climate: assessment of, 17–28; and climate continuum, 23–24; and climate survey, 17; and climate survey tools and tips, 19–22; and information needed by network, 18, 23; for network forming, 25–27; among potential members, 27–28; for women, 24–25

Company environment: assessment of, 14–15; and getting off the ground, 16–17; and gauging potential support for women's network, 15–16; and management's support, 16; risk factor in, 17; and support of human resources, 16; and women's support, 15–16

Constituencies, major, of networks, 15–16, 60

Conversation, informal, 19, 26

Corporate employees, going beyond, 33

Corporate women's groups, 32

Creating Women's Networks (Catalyst), 159

D

Dain Rauscher, 4, 55–56

Data, quantitative versus qualitative, 18

Disbanding network: common reasons for, 152–153; and litigation, 153; questions to be asked before, 153–155

Diversity, 14, 134–135

Diversity councils, 81–82

Dow Chemical, 6, 103–104, 172

Dow Chemical WIN Change process, 172

Dow Chemical Women's Innovation Network, 103

Dual-career marriages, 34

Dual purpose data, 23

E

Eastman Kodak, 6, 157–158, 175–178. *See also* Kodak employees briefing book; Women's Forum of Kodak Employees

Economic downturns, 149–151

Effectiveness, defining and measuring, 91–92, 96–97, 102, 106

Elections, 122–123

Environment. *See* Company environment

Euronet (Kimberly-Clark), 180

Event managers, 87. *See also* Networking events

Events and programs. *See* Networking events

Exclusiveness, versus inclusiveness, 30, 32, 34

Executives, key questions for, 26–27

External challenges: and changes in senior leadership, 151–152; and economic downturns, 149–151

F

Feedback mechanisms, 52

Flexible work arrangements, 24–25

Focus Asia (Kimberly-Clark), 180

Focus groups, 20

Follow-up surveys, 91

Ford, 5

Formal surveys, 21–22

Funding, 123–124

G

Gay and Lesbian Network (Kimberly-Clark), 179–180

Gender, 34

Geographic expansion, 33

Global Partnership Network for Women, 9–10, 53

H

Hewlett-Packard, 5

High-visibility activities: and effec-
tive publicity, 101–102; involving senior leaders in, 102; key to, 99–100; and meeting members' needs, 100–101; reference list of, 100

Hoffman-LaRoche women's network, 119

Human Resource data, analysis of, 20–21

Human Resources: building support in, 73–80; checklist for building support in, 84; and definition of lines, 74; and diversity councils, 81–82; inclusion of, on network committees, 79–80; and men in the company, 82–83; and other employee networks, 81; and other employees, 82; strategies for building relationship with, 75; support continuum chart for, 76–78; and women outside the network, 83; working with, 79

Human Resources professionals, 74

I

IBM, 5

Inclusiveness, versus exclusiveness, 30, 32, 34, 126–129

Individual meetings, 61

Information, 88, 95

Initiatives, at Texas Instruments, 43

Initiators: and assessing company climate, 17–28; and assessment of company environment, 14–15; and climate survey tools and tips, 19–22; first steps for, 14–17; and gauging potential support, 15–16; and getting off the ground, 16–17; individual aspects of, 13–14

Intensity, 89, 114

Internal challenges: and common internal challenges, 142–143; and membership needs and interests, 144; and obsolete membership criteria, 145–146; and reasons for low participation, 144–145

Internal network systems. *See* Network organization

Issue-focused committees, 49–50

J

Junkins, J., 43

K

Kimberly-Clark, 2, 136, 179–180
Kimberly-Clark employee networks, 179–180
Kodak diversity office, 157
Kodak employees briefing book, 175–178
Kraft African American Council, 35
Kraft Foods, 6, 35

L

LAND. *See* Latin American Network for Diversity
Latin American Network for Diversity (LAND), 180
Leaders: need for, 45–46; roles for, 47–48; rotating system for, 48
Leadership, changes in, 151–152
Leadership structure, 45
Leadership succession, 122–123
Leadership pool, 125–126
Leadership team, presentations to, 64–66
"Let's Talk Business" dinners (3M), 118
Leveraging relationships, 66–67, 72–73
Litigation, 153
Low participation, 144–145
Lucent Technologies, 44

M

Management, advising. *See* Advising activities
Management liaison, 67
McDonald's Corporation, 6, 33
McDonald's Spouse Certification Program, 33
McGraw-Hill, 2, 6, 92
MCI, 44
Members, potential: identification of, 30–35; key questions for, 27–28
Membership: and coalition building, 138; and connecting with

other employee needs, 135–137; and ensuring diverse membership, 134–135; and helping other women in the company, 138–139; including senior women in, 133–134; and inclusive versus exclusive membership, 30, 32; and increasing the leadership pool, 125–126; and maintaining a cohesive and inclusive network, 126–129; and membership building, 131–139; and membership perks, 130; and recognizing successes, 130–131; and team-building phases, 127–129
Membership meetings, 120–122
Merck, 6
Middle management: building support in, 67–73; and education and communication, 68–71; strategies to leverage relationship with, 72–73; support continuum chart for, 69–71; and support from top, 71–72
Mission statement: creation of, 35–36; elements of, 36
Motorola, 6, 44

N

Name, importance of, 52. *See also* Network organization
NEON (Kimberly-Clark). *See* New Employee Opportunity Network (NEON)
Network: checklist for, 28; four aspects of, 13–14; gathering information for, 14–17; mission statement for, 35–36; need for, 13–28; organization of, 45–58; roles and goals for, 29–37
Network agenda: checklist for, 37; and common activities and purposes chart, 38–42; creation of, 36–37
Network effectiveness: and lack of clear next steps, 148; and lack of leadership, 148–149; and network redefinition, 147; and unattainable goals, 146–148
Network maintenance: and basic housekeeping, 120–124; check-

list for, 141; and evaluating effectiveness, 139–141; and membership, 124–131; and membership building, 131–139
Network members: function of, 33–34; gender of, 34; identification of, 30–35; level of, 31–32; location of, 32–33
Network of Networks (Kimberly-Clark), 136
Network organization: checklist for, 54; and committees, 49–50; and communications strategies, 51–53; and leadership roles, 47–48; and putting structure in place, 46–47
Network success factors: and clear objective, 86–87; and effective communication of event and purpose, 86; and key to network success, 29–30; and member needs, 86; and network activities, 86–87; and senior leaders, 87
Network-focused committees, 50
Networking activities. *See* Networking events
Networking events: and advising management and human resources, 107–115; and career development events, 93–98; checklist for, 115; common goals for, 88–89; common groups included in, 89; defining and measuring effectiveness of, 91–92; and effective publicity, 91; and high-visibility activities, 99–102; involving company's senior leaders in, 92–93; and meeting members needs, 90–91; reference list of, 90; and sharing of information, 88; and success factors, 86–87; and support of goals and mission, 85–115; and tips for event managers, 87; and wider community, 105–106
New Approach to Flexibility, A: Managing the Work/Time Equation (Catalyst), 15
New Employee Opportunity Network (NEON), 136, 179
New members' kits, 133

O

One-to-one programs, 95–96

P

Partnering, 136–137
Partnership, concept of, 94
Persuasion, 112
Philip Morris, 35
Power, 57, 59–84
Procter & Gamble, 5
Publicity, effective, 91, 96, 101–102, 106

Q

Quantitative, versus qualitative data, 18

R

Risk factor, 17

S

Senior management: building support in, 59–67; dos and don'ts in advisement of, 64; and informal opportunities for meeting with, 66; key questions for, 26–27; and management liaison, 67; and presentations to the leadership team, 64–66; specific strategies for building relationships with, 61–66; strategies to leverage relationship with, 66–67; support continuum chart for, 62–63
Senior women, 133–134
Skills, 13
Steering committees, 14, 46, 47–48
Subcommittees, 46
Subteams, 129
Succession plan, 48, 122–123
Support: basic srategies for enlist-

ing, 83; building, 59–84; checklist for, 84; constituency groups for, 60; and diversity councils, 81–82; and Human Resources, 73–80; key questions for, 60; of men in company, 82–83; and middle management, 67–73; and other employees, 82; and other groups, 80, 81; and senior management, 61–67; of women outside network, 83

T

"Take Our Daughters to Work" day, 87, 99, 100, 102
Team-building phases, 127–129
Texas Instruments, 2, 6, 43–44
3M, 2, 6, 117–118, 119
Toastmasters, 98
Tools, range of, 51
Two Careers, One Marriage (Catalyst), 15, 34

W

WIN. *See* Women's Interactive Network
Women in Management Network (McGraw-Hill), 92
Women and Men in Power, 53
Women in Operations (WIO), 35
Women Operators Network (WON), 33
Women in Power (WIP), 53
"Women on Wall Street" (Global Partnership for Women), 10
Women-only activities, 34
Women's Advisory Committee (WAC), 117–118, 119. *See also* 3M
Women's Forum of Kodak Employees: and CEO support, 157–158; guiding principles of, 176; mission of, 175; and 1998

initiatives, 177–178; organizational structure of, 176; vision of, 175
Women's History Month, 99, 100, 102
Women's Interactive Network (WIN), 180
Women's Opportunity Workshops (Dow Chemical), 103
Women's Workplace Networks Survey: and activities for women's networks, 167; about companies responding to, 162–163; companies with women's networks, 163–164; and employee networks, 162; and frequency and level of women's networks, 164; and groups served by women's networks, 167–168; and initiators of women's networks, 164–165; and membership of women's networks, 165; and most important issues, 166–167; and negative responses to women's networks, 169–170; and positive responses to women's networks, 168–169; and reasons for forming women's networks, 166; and relationships among employee networks, 166; and resources provided by company and women's networks, 165–166; respondents to, 161–162; and roles played by women's networks, 168
Work/life balance, 24, 34

X

Xerox, 6

Y

Young Women's Christian Association (YWCA), 98, 106

RESEARCH REPORTS

Catalyst research reports are available for purchase, and you can find out more about us and what we do on the World Wide Web. Feel free to call on Catalyst for more information.

Address:

CATALYST
120 Wall Street, 5th floor
New York, NY 10005

Phone: 212-514-7600

E-mail: info@catalystwomen.org

Web site: http://www.catalystwomen.org